Remember The Ways

One Woman's Journey

By

Helen L. Griffin

Someday I'm going to write a book,
I thought to myself.
But I don't know enough yet to write a book.
I have to live first.
Now I've lived.
Now I submit to you this book.

Copyright © 2013 by Helen L. Griffin

Remember The Ways:
One Woman's Journey
by Helen L. Griffin

Printed in the United States of America

ISBN 9781628390438

All rights reserved solely by the author. The author guarantees all contents are original and do not infringe upon the legal rights of any other person or work. No part of this book may be reproduced in any form without the permission of the author. The views expressed in this book are not necessarily those of the publisher.

Unless otherwise indicated, Bible quotations are taken from the New King James Version (NKJV). Copyright © 1982 by Thomas Nelson, Inc. Used by permission. All rights reserved.

Scripture marked LB is taken from *The Living Bible,* copyright © 1971. Used by permission of Tyndale House Publishers, Inc., Wheaton, Illinois 60189. All rights reserved.

Scripture marked NASB is taken from the New American Standard Bible®, Copyright © 1960, 1962, 1963, 1968, 1971, 1972, 1973, 1975, 1977, 1995 by The Lockman Foundation. Used by permission.

www.xulonpress.com

In Honor of
Dorothy Odell Smith Scantling
1921-2010

My mother who used to tell me,
"I can count on you; you are responsible."
Likewise, I could count on her to be true and
honorable,
faithful and diligent, hardworking and caring,
like the prudent woman of Proverbs 31.

She always had a song, and we sometimes
sang together.
One of her favorites began:

As I travel through this pilgrim land
There is a Friend who walks with me,
Leads me safely through the sinking sand,
It is the Christ of Calvary.
This would be my prayer, dear Lord, each day
To help me do the best I can,

*For I need Thy light to guide me day and night,
Blessed Jesus, hold my hand.*

It was the song she and I sang
the last two times we sang together.

*

DEDICATED TO

My children and my children's children

And to *you* the reader

Table of Contents

Introduction xi

Chapter 1   The 1940s and 1950s
From Sugar Grove to Chicago 13

Chapter 2   The 1960s
Marriage and Motherhood in Mexico. 44

Chapter 3   The 1970s
Of Teaching and of Traveling 80

Chapter 4   The 1980s
My Dark Night of the Soul 152

Chapter 5   The 1990s
"The City of Eternal Springtime". 206

Chapter 6   The 2000s
The Desires of Our Hearts 252

Epilogue
Back to My Beginnings 267

***REMEMBER ALL THE WAY WHICH THE
LORD YOUR GOD HAS LED YOU***
... testing you, to know what was in
your heart
(Deut. 8:2 NASB)

***Walking with my little Mexican friend Josie.
Parlier, California 1943***

Introduction

My older brother Jimmy and cousin Joanne had let the air out of the tires on Daddy's coupe parked by the lemon trees in Parlier, California.

A lively disagreement ensued over who was responsible. "Ask Helen," said Aunt Laverne. "She always tells the truth."

That's the first thing I knew about myself: that I always told the truth.

Another thing I knew: I loved the dirt under the lemon trees. I would get myself one of those flat Mason jar lids my mother used for canning and scrape up the dirt and eat it. The young Satterfield girl who looked after us would give me a whack on the bottom and take away my lid. I would go back around the house, through the kitchen door, pull open a drawer, find another lid and get back to my business.

The other thing I knew was that I loved my daddy more than anything. He would come back from the grape arbors where he and my mother had been picking the clusters all day, catch me up in his sinewy arms, and ask, "How much do you love me?"

I would stretch my arms wide, measuring how much, and then throw them around his neck, declaring, "I love you a great big ole gob!"

I loved truth, I loved nutritious lemon-flavored dirt, and I loved my daddy.

* * *

Over sixty years had passed since these events in California and I knew it was time to start writing this story. I mentioned it to a friend in a letter.

She wrote back, "Who told you to write a book? You're supposed to be loving people."

I was taken aback at first. Nobody had told me to write one. I had just always known I would.

I had written a number of small books just for my children and grandchildren, and for my mother and sister; and I had written one about my dad, for my mother.

The stories were about them because I loved them.

I would write because of love. That's why I write this for you.

Chapter 1

The 1940s and 1950s
From Sugar Grove to Chicago

My parents, James and Dorothy Scantling, were married on April 9, 1938, by Mr. Townsend, the justice of the peace in Sugar Grove, Arkansas, where they were born and grew up. Daddy was twenty and Mother was sixteen. They had not been brought up in church, but she tells about attending a revival meeting when she was a child and going forward to shake the preacher's hand.

When my brother Jimmy was born, Mother almost died. Heavy rains made all the creeks around Sugar Grove overflow their banks, covering the bridges and blocking access to the nearby towns of Booneville or Magazine making it impossible to bring a doctor. Jimmy was born at 5:00 on Sunday afternoon February 19, 1939, but Mother, unconscious and having convulsions, was not even aware she had given birth to a son.

When old Dr. Hedrick finally made it through on Tuesday morning, he said, "She has kidney poisoning.

I'll give her this injection to stop the convulsions, but when the effects wear off she will die. There's nothing more I can do." He headed out the door with, "Don't call me back." Daddy threw himself down by her bed and begged God to spare her. And God did. The doctor was amazed she had recovered, but he ordered them, "Don't have any more children. If you do, you must wait at least six or seven years." *I'm glad they didn't obey him, else I wouldn't have been born the following year.*

Aunt Nova told me the night I was born she prayed for the *young* Doctor Hedrick to be the one to come and deliver me because the older Doctor Hedrick had left my mother to die. I can't blame him though. He only did what he could and then God did what only *He* could.

When I was six months old, special meetings were being held at the Mt. Sinai Assembly of God Church in Sugar Grove, about two miles from where we lived. My mother wrote,

> We started going. James had prayed for me when Jimmy was born, and believed with all his heart that the Lord heard and answered his prayer for my healing, and I had gone to the altar when I was going to school, but we hadn't been really sincere about living for the Lord. Now it was much different. We had truly given our lives over to the Lord, and there is nothing in this world to compare with the peace, joy, and happiness that was in our hearts.

We were without a car but didn't mind in the least the two-mile walk to church, James carrying Jimmy and I carrying Helen. A short time later we were both baptized in Sugar Creek's "Ole Baptizin' Hole."

When our little family of four later moved to Ione to be near my dad's sawmill site, he bought his first car, a 1929 Model-A Ford and drove us fifteen miles every Sunday back to the church in Sugar Grove. Later we moved to Grayson, a good-sized saw-milling community, to a pretty little house on a hill and started going to the Grayson Assembly of God Church. Their roots, and mine, were in those two Assembly of God churches, and from there flow some of my earliest memories

California, 1943. James with Jimmy and Alton, Dorothy with Helen

When my younger brother was born, we left Arkansas for migrant years in California from 1942-45, Arizona in 1946, and Oklahoma in 1947, with stints back in the home state between each move, traveling the completed Route 66 which stretched from Chicago all the way to Los Angeles.

During those times back in Arkansas, my two younger sisters were born.

By the time we ended up in Thayer, Illinois, in November of 1948, not too far from the coal mines where he found work, my dad had wandered far spiritually. Thayer was a small community of four hundred people with a Methodist Church, grade school, town hall, grocery, general store with post office—and a tavern that I hated to go into on Saturdays to collect for my paper route, the *St. Louis Post-Dispatch*. Joe Karaffa, a classmate, told me I shouldn't mind, because my dad went in there, but I didn't want to believe him.

In April of 1950 things took a seasonal turn for the better, and my dad bought a 1939 four-door Plymouth and took our family of seven to the Virden Assembly of God Church two miles south of us. Rev. George Ankarlo and his wife Isabelle were both dynamic preachers and teachers. At the altar my dad "prayed through," as they called it, and had a total change of direction in life. Living for the Lord and going to church became the priority for the whole family, and James led the way.

Our pastor and his family. *The Ankarlos with their first son George Wayne.*

On Mother's Day, May 14, 1950, I climbed into the backseat of the Plymouth for the two-mile ride to church, with no idea of what this day would mean in my life. Instead of the regular service Isabelle Ankarlo surprised us with a flannelgraph story for the children. As I watched and listened my spiritual eyes were opened—like a curtain parting. For the first time I understood the gospel story of my sinfulness and God's design for my salvation through the sacrifice of Jesus on the cross. I led the pack that headed down to the altar that morning. Sister Ankarlo knelt and prayed with me. I remember a sense of kneeling at Jesus' cross, where He washed away my sin, came into my heart and made me His forever. Riding back home in the backseat of the car at noonday, I pondered what had happened. *I don't feel any special emotion*, I thought to myself, *but I know that Jesus lives in me now and forever*. That assurance has never left me throughout my lifetime.

Deeper than emotion, more certain than intellect ... in the depths of my spirit I knew.

My fourth-grade school picture

We grew strong in our faith under the teaching of the Ankarlos in that little church.

We never missed Sunday school, Sunday morning worship, Sunday evening children's church, Sunday night service, Wednesday night Bible study, and Saturday night "Christ's Ambassadors." At least six times a week we were taught the Scriptures, plus we had a yearly revival, a camp meeting and vacation Bible school. Sunday school picnics, church suppers, and Sunday afternoons of going calling on other families in the church were like glue that bound the church family together. Sometimes we visited Daddy's buddies from the coal mine so he could witness to them of his faith and invite them to come to Christ.

One afternoon during a picnic at the Pattons' farm with its large pond, Sister Ankarlo dashed up to me and said, "You have received Jesus. Do you want to be baptized now?"

"Yes!" I said, and she went around gathering up others also who had not yet been baptized. We waded out where she and her husband immersed all of us, including Aunt Faye and Uncle Howard, who had recently moved up to Thayer.

In children's church, before each Sunday evening service, Sister Ankarlo told us a Bible story plus a missionary story. It was then I would see myself as that missionary standing under the tree teaching the group seated on benches. One winter evening as some of us were milling around the pot-bellied coal stove at the back of the church, an elderly man asked me, "What are you going to be, young lady, when you grow up?"

I'd never expressed it before, but I replied, "I want to go away to Bible school and study to be a missionary."

I asked my mother to please let me have the flannelgraph figures from the lessons she taught preschoolers on Sunday morning. "I can't just give them to you," she said. "I'll have to ask the pastor's wife if it's all right." She was given permission, and I used them to teach my younger brother and two younger sisters the Bible stories. When my dad became Sunday school superintendent, I was so proud of him, just as I was of my mother for being a teacher. I used to sit by him in church and look up into his face as the Bible was being read and the sermon preached, marveling as I watched him drinking it in, understanding it. He helped me win a *Hurlbut's Story of the Bible* in a Sunday school contest. I read it all the way through to my siblings and drilled them with the questions at the back. They learned all the stories, too, and could answer all the questions.

Ray Davis was a superb junior Sunday school teacher. Once he let me teach the story of the Good Samaritan with my flannelgraph figures. He and his wife Joyce took us places like the St. Louis Zoo where I got to ride an elephant. One summer day they took the class swimming at a dam outside Palmyra. It was called Terry Park, and our family several years later would actually come to live there.

The elderly gentleman who had asked me what I wanted to be encouraged me to memorize chapters of the Bible and recite them in church, so I did a lot of memorizing. Later a lady from a nearby town recruited me to memorize speeches for the *Woman's Christian Temperance Union* and took me with her to recite them at different functions in the area. During those four years in the Virden church, we flourished under the leadership of the Ankarlos and Davises and mourned our loss when they relocated south to Maryville, Illinois.

I remember discontent in the church as time went by and a new pastor could not be agreed on. Nobody could measure up to the Ankarlos. Several came to "try out." One day a powerful preacher appeared, and everybody wanted him, but he had said, "If you vote on me, I will not come." They voted unanimously for him, and he refused to come. Later the Rev. and Mrs. Robert B. Byers, an older couple without children took the position. They were as low-key and retiring as the Ankarlos were dynamic and full of life.

Soon afterward we moved to Virden, closer to the church location but farther from God. Daddy's interest dwindled. He was drifting, and I wondered how much the unsettledness at church had to do with it, and what also had actually happened. He came home one day with a television—an ominous sign to my mother, who hit the ceiling. He was bringing the world into our home. Daddy won out, and the television stayed. Mother put tight restrictions on what we could watch—just *Howdy Doody*. My brothers clamored to watch westerns, but she would not hear of guns and shooting in our house.

We moved to Palmyra my eighth grade year, where no Assembly of God Church existed, so we joined the Baptist Church, but Daddy didn't attend with us. He became a local hero overnight upon finding a little boy and his dog lost deep in the woods. He was one in a party of three hundred men searching the woods for eight hours. His new buddies celebrated him at the local tavern. He later became a Mason and begged me to accept their invitation to join the Rainbow Girls. I asked my pastor, Rev. Clyde Masten, who said, "Never!" The following year we moved out to Terry Park as caretakers of the grounds. By that time Daddy's drinking was escalating.

The passion for missions was always in my heart. In the AG I'd heard continually about missions. Ray Davis had even said once, "Maybe someday Helen will be a missionary to China." I liked that, but those were the days of the communist regime coming into power and the country becoming closed to missions. I knew with certainty I did not want to go to Africa! I had read of missionaries there who were required to send their children away at age six to boarding school. I could never send my child away at such a tender age to a distant boarding school for missionaries' children. I wouldn't go to Africa! One evening in youth group at the Baptist church, the subject of missions came up. Afterward, I spoke to my pastor. "God has called me to be a missionary," I said. I was surprised as tears rose to my eyes at the depth of emotion I felt.

"That's wonderful," he said. "Here's what we'll do. One Sunday morning soon, I'll invite any young people to come forward who want to dedicate their lives for full-time Christian service." He later gave the call. I went forward. My mother wasn't there that morning, so the next day Rev. Masten arrived at Terry Park, knocking on our door. We sat down in the kitchen.

"Did you tell your mother what you did yesterday?" he asked.

"No," I said. I was sorry I hadn't. I don't know what I was thinking—that mothers already knew everything and didn't need to be told?

He loaned me two inspiring biographies to read—the life of C. T. Studd and the life of D. L. Moody. His wife, Shirley, came out to Terry Park almost every day that summer to mentor me as we golfed together. I missed their godly influence when they left to take another church. The American Baptist Convention had a conference on missions, and the ladies of the church took me along with them. I was greatly challenged by the life of Adoniram Judson, who had gone at the beginning of modern missions to Burma as the convention's very first foreign missionary. I was also impressed with the sessions led by a home missionary to the Native Americans.

My dad held down three jobs: working full-time in the coal mine, running his own coal delivery business, and overseeing the care and upkeep of Terry Park with its golf course, lakes, rodeo and horse grounds, and two community buildings for renting out—and he drank more and more.

I was fifteen when I skipped lunch at school one day and dashed over to the Baptist parsonage to meet the new pastor, Rev. F. Roy Parker, and his wife

Irene. They were a childless older couple, and I liked them immediately. Her laughter sounded like bells coming up out of a well.

"I wish I were in your place," I blurted out.

"Why?" they asked.

"Because you get to have fellowship all the time, all you want, with other Christians in the church."

"Don't you believe it," Brother Parker said with sadness. "We have not met any yet who are seeking that." I was shocked. I knew I hadn't found any in my high school. I was always looking for a turned-on Christian friend. I'd expected, though, that among the grown-ups there would be many spiritual giants.

Then I brought up my real reason for bursting in on them. "What's going to happen to my dad?" I asked Brother Parker. "He used to follow Jesus, and now he doesn't."

"A believer who drifts away will be disciplined by the Lord," he explained to me. "I believe if he has truly been born again, God will bring him back before he dies." I grabbed onto that hope because I knew my dad had been a real, on-fire Christian the four years we were in the Virden church.

The summer before my senior year of high school, I searched for Bible schools. One day, sorting through some Sunday school material given to my mother by Mrs. Gordon in the church, I found a *Moody Monthly* magazine. I'd never seen one before. On the back cover was a full-page announcement of Moody Bible Institute in Chicago. I hopped on my bicycle and rode into town to see the Parkers. Holding up the magazine with the back cover showing, I said, "Do you know anything about this school to recommend it or not?"

"We most certainly do!" he said. "Mrs. Parker and I graduated from there in 1934." I submitted an inquiry to MBI, as I had been doing with other possibilities I discovered, in my diligent search for the right school.

Easter 1957. *Seated:* **Mother, Linda, Daddy.** *Standing:* **Joyce, Helen, Jimmy, Alton.**

My good friend Janice Overbey invited me to her church in the nearby town of Modesto one evening to hear a missionary couple from West Pakistan. Vern and Wanda Rock were home on furlough after five years with TEAM (The Evangelical Alliance Mission). They donned traditional dress from Pakistan and talked about their ministry. Afterward,

I went up to Wanda and said, "God has called me to be a missionary."

"That's wonderful," she exclaimed. "Why don't you come and spend a weekend with me? We can talk more." She gave me her address in nearby Girard, and said, "In fact, how about this weekend? My husband has to be traveling, and I'd enjoy having company. It'll just be me at home with our two little boys."

First, she served two cups of hot tea, the kind she had learned to enjoy in Pakistan. It was a new experience for me, sipping hot tea from a dainty teacup. We sat at her table and talked while the boys played in the yard. I told her about my recent inquiry into Moody Bible Institute, and she smiled. "That's one of the top three Bible schools," she said.

I asked her how long it had taken her to learn the new language. When she said she was still learning, I thought *What? I want to learn the language immediately so I can get on with the work and teaching*. Of course, I had no concept of the complexity of learning a Central Asian language with its strange alphabet and the long hours and grueling discipline it takes. Then I asked her what she did all day as a missionary. I expected to hear of a life filled with exciting activity. "It's very much the same as a wife and mother here at home," she said, "the everyday chores of caring for family." *What?* I thought again. *I want to have a family, but I also want to be busy with missionary work.* Later I learned how work in a Muslim country is vastly different—especially for a woman—than I had ever imagined.

She took me across town to meet her parents. Her father, Mr. Walden, showed me his library and loaned me *A Passion for Souls* by Oswald J. Smith, which greatly impacted my life. The weekend was so special for me. *Wanda Rock was the first foreign missionary I ever met.*

I applied to Moody Bible Institute, and was ecstatic the following January on receiving a long white envelope with my acceptance. But that summer my mother said, "Helen, your dad and I have talked this over, and there is no way we can help send you to school. I'm afraid you're going to have to give up your idea of going."

"There won't be any problem," I assured her. "I can work my way through."

My pastor and his wife offered to drive me in their Studebaker the 150 miles north to Chicago to their alma mater from twenty-four years before. When I hopped into the backseat, there sat Thelma Vance. "What are you doing here?" I asked, surprised. I had just driven out to her parents' farm three miles from us and dropped off my cat "Moonlight" with three baby kittens. My mother had said I couldn't go away till I found another home for those cats. It was a surprise to everybody that timid Thelma would break away and go to the big city.

On the drive up, Rev. Parker said to me, "Helen, while you're at Moody, we expect you're going to meet a nice young man who will ask you to marry him. But we would like you to finish your schooling first."

"Oh, yes," I agreed. "That's what I intend to do. I don't want to drop out to get married."

They helped me check in and then sneaked up to the accounting department to make a $100 deposit on my bill. I had no idea they were doing it! Since Moody is tuition free, all I had to pay for that semester was my textbooks. Beginning the second semester, I was able to work to cover my room and board and any other expenses. My mother's fears about finances were unfounded. That day the Parkers helped Thelma get a job in housekeeping with living quarters across the street, while I checked into my dorm on the tenth floor of Houghton Hall. To my delight, across the hall I found Pam Witts from England, who had already been a missionary in Africa for one term. I rushed her downstairs to meet the Parkers. "Look! I've already made my first friend—and she's a missionary!"

On one of my trips home from Moody, Mother pulled me aside. "Your dad's drinking is way out of hand," she confided. This was not easy for her to say. She had never spoken negatively about him to me before. But with heavy heart, she was looking for help. "Every time he comes home drunk now, I calculate how much he has spent on alcohol and take that amount from the cash box in the concession stand and put it aside. He's going to be surprised to see how much it comes to. Maybe that will shock him into changing." More than anything, she was concerned for his soul. We knelt beside their bed that day and claimed together the verse, "If two of you shall agree together as touching anything you shall ask, it shall be done for you." We didn't know it would take twenty years for that prayer to be answered, but we agreed together. We asked God to set Daddy free from liquor and bring him back to His path.

I had a list of qualities I wanted in a husband. I had chosen traits of men I admired most and put them all together to build this ideal man. But there were two absolute requisites:

- He would love God above all else.
- He would be the spiritual leader in our home.

I saw Dick first, without his seeing me. I had dropped into one of the before-lunch prayer meetings where George Verwer, the young missions leader, stood before a huge map of Mexico. On the far side of the room, I saw Dick slumped in a chair, wearing a shirt that hadn't been ironed. *He needs a wife*, I thought to myself, little knowing I would be the one! I heard George refer to Dick as having been to Mexico that past Christmas. We didn't meet until May 31, 1959, one week before school was out. I had come walking into the dining hall that Sunday noon after returning from my assignment of teaching a teenage girls' Sunday school class at Ravensbrook Baptist Church across the city. My first year at Moody was coming to an end, and I had never entered before from the men's dormitory end of the campus. But that day, Ron, another student with an assignment at the same church, offered me a ride back in his car. He parked at the men's entrance.

Since it was Sunday and we didn't have assigned seating, I chose an empty place and sat down. It turned out to be at Dick's table—the second time now I had walked unknowingly into his territory. Recognizing him from the Mexico meeting, I said, "You've been to Mexico, haven't you? Tell me about Mexico." He told me about the team in Monterrey that past Christmas and of his plans to go down again during the three-month summer vacation. When I stood to leave, he asked for my name and jotted it down. That evening I noted in my small green diary: "Talked to Dick Griffin at dinner." Then I wrote home to my mother, "I met Dick today." When she asked me what he was like, I said, "He loves the Lord more than anything else."

In a student body of one thousand, it was highly unlikely that we would encounter each other again that last week of school. But Friday night graduation exercises at Moody Church found me again, without realizing it, in his sphere of action. I came in with my friend Anita Post and at her insistence accompanied her up to the balcony. I never would have chosen the balcony. Dick, assigned to usher in the very section we entered, was the one to seat us! When Anita noticed his interest in me, she did a disappearing act at the end, leaving me abandoned for him to walk me the eight blocks back to school! "We're supposed to get people to pray for us while we're in Mexico," Dick said as we walked back to Houghton Hall. "Would you be one of my prayer partners?" I agreed, and he carefully wrote down my name and summer address to send me reports. We were both to be in Monterreys—he in Monterrey, Mexico, and I in Monterey, Massachusetts, at the New England Keswick girls' camp.

My cabin full of teenage girls was excited at mail call on June 23 to see that I had a letter from Mexico. I had to tell them everything I knew about Dick; then they clamored to see a picture of him. "Make a deal with you," I said. "I'll show you his school photo when you get my tennis shoes down out of the tree!"
I wouldn't have had a picture of him had I not packed my fresh-off-the-press yearbook in my camping gear. "He's cute!" one of the girls exclaimed. Not even *I* knew it then, but they really would have swooned if they had seen his high school annuals plastered with his picture as Mr. Greenville High School ... Most Versatile Boy ... football star ... track star ...
I answered Dick's two letters that summer using a stationery pad with Scripture verses at the top. The second time he wrote and I replied, the verse said, "May the Lord watch between me and thee when we are absent one from the other." It turned out he liked that very much and had carried it in his pocket to read every day, wondering if perhaps I felt the same way he did.

When we showed up on registration day back at Moody for the fall term I saw him across the room with that letter sticking out of his shirt pocket. *He must be interested in me*, I thought, *to be carrying my letter around.* But any illusions I may have had vanished as weeks went by and he never got in touch with me. No letter, no note, no visit, no call—absolutely nothing. A whole month went by, and Dick did not contact me at all. Actually, it turned out he had made a vow to the Lord that he would not date another girl until he knew she was the one.

Meanwhile, he spent the time praying, particularly concerned about our age difference. I was still eighteen, and he had already turned twenty-seven. Was he robbing the cradle? When he was a senior in high school, I would have been in fourth grade! I was praying, too, during that month, often up on the roof of Houghton Hall, only one flight up because I already lived on the tenth floor. I sought the quiet beneath the sky. It was there I felt forced to accept that he was not interested. Under the stars I surrendered him to the Lord and told God I was willing to go as a single missionary to the field.

On Friday afternoon of the first week of October, Dick finally decided that the least he could do was find out what I thought about the age difference. But when he arrived at Houghton Hall desk to ask permission to talk to me and they buzzed my room, I was not in. I had spent the afternoon in the library on fifth floor of Crowell Hall. When I got into the elevator to go down, the operator said, "It's raining outside. Do you want to get off at ground floor, or do you want to take the tunnel? It'll be dry in the tunnel."

"Ground floor, please," I said. "I like the rain." That's where Dick and I met, walking toward each other in the rain. If I had chosen the tunnel, we would have missed each other. I invited him to the social room on second floor of Houghton Hall. He went straight to what was troubling him—that he was too old for me. "That's no problem," I said. "I've always thought the man should be a bit older." (I didn't tell him, but my best friend, Ester Poole, had said I should not date him, that he was too old for me; but I had asked my mother, and she said that he wasn't.)

He practically asked me that same evening to marry him, by saying he would not be able to buy an engagement ring, explaining how the group going down to Mexico was committed to saving every penny to get the gospel out. I told him that was all right with me. We talked all the way through supper, neither of us wanting to leave and go to the dining hall. It was "State Night," when everyone sat according to his or her home state. "It doesn't matter what state we're from," Dick said. "I'm from Mississippi but came to Moody after living a year in Texas, so I wouldn't know which table to choose." I told him I was born in Arkansas but had lived in California, Arizona, and Oklahoma before moving to Illinois. Illinois would already have too many tables. So we continued talking all the way through mealtime.

"Would you like to accompany me to Moody Church tomorrow night for the missions conference?" he asked before we said goodnight. That would be our first date.

I was cleaning my dormitory room the next morning when the hall telephone rang. It was Leslie Lamar, a boy I used to like in eighth grade who never gave up. "I'm in Chicago for the day," he said. "I'm in the navy and have this day free. Can I see you?"

Reluctantly, I agreed to go walking with him down to Lake Michigan. I took Thelma along. When it came time for my date with Dick, I passed Leslie to Thelma. He accompanied her to Moody Church and was not happy but had no choice. That Saturday I went out with Dick for the very *first* time—and the very *last* time ever with Leslie.

I made another change too. The year before I had caught Chicago's public transit every Saturday night with a group of students to the home of Arthur and Hilda Matthews, veteran missionaries to China. (*Green Leaf in Drought Time,* written by Isabel Kuhn, had featured their dramatic escape from China at the time of the revolution.) We prayed for the China Inland Mission and its uprooted members, who were in the process of being relocated to other countries of Southeast Asia. The mission was becoming known then as the Overseas Missionary Fellowship. The Matthews were very hospitable, receiving us into their home regularly and hosting a mid-term retreat there. I never missed the Saturday evening meetings. One night, out of the blue, while he was speaking, Arthur Matthews looked at me and said, "Helen, when you're in the boiling pot, don't try to get out." *I would have a reason to remember that many, many years later.*

China was always on my heart. I had read all of Hudson Taylor's copious writings about the beginnings of the China Inland Mission. I can still see myself pulling those heavy volumes from the library shelves. They comprised my thousand pages of required reading that semester for missions class. But I switched—giving up CIM fellowship meetings for Spanish Club and the orientation sessions for the group preparing to go to Mexico during Christmas break.

On November 14, 1959, as we returned from a stroll along Lake Michigan, Dick formally proposed by saying, "Would you be my help-meet?" I thought those were the words I heard, but I pondered them as traffic zoomed down Chicago Avenue and we neared the school. I finally concluded that he had indeed asked me to marry him.

"Yes, I want to marry you," I said, "but—would you be willing to wait until I graduate?" I told him about my commitment to the Parkers to finish school first. Of course, he would wait! He told me he had already waited so many years for the right one that another nineteen months would not be long. The night was cold. He took my hand and slipped it into the pocket of the brown wool overcoat he'd inherited from his dad.

After saying good night in the lobby of Houghton Hall, I glanced at the elevator going up. Then I looked at the stairs and chose the stairs, as I often did. The ten flights were not the same this time, though. I had the sensation of actually floating! The euphoria carried me up to my dorm room, where I discovered my roommate, Cora, was already sound asleep. But I've got to tell somebody this wonderful news! I can't keep it to myself! I knocked on the door across the hall, where Carol, the student rep, lived. "Carol! The most wonderful thing has happened! Dick has asked me to marry him!" Carol's beaming face reflected my own joy there in the late night stillness of the women's dorm. *Some joys are too good to keep. They have to be shared.*

Crossing the border into Mexico that Christmas was like entering another world. Even the soil and the sky had a different feel. Curious brown eyes stared at the pale-faced *gringa* recently arrived from snowy Chicago, and she stared back. There were no signs of Christmas except manger scenes on beds of moss, no other Christmas sights, sounds, smells, tastes, or sensations. My team leader, Dr. Bob Cook, our Spanish professor at Moody, was low-key, in contrast to our dynamic, fast-forward, let-out-all-the-stops director George Verwer, Jr., who plunked us off at the home of Baldemar Aguilar, our co-laborer, and headed on farther south with the rest of the teams. How would we function as a team without the "high" George kept us on? The stillness was almost eerie, like the wake of a tornado. Sitting in a stuffed chair at the entrance to Mrs. Aguilar's living room sat Fern Tillotson. I became impressed that Christmas by the prayer life and zeal in witnessing of Fern, who had been a missionary to the Jewish community in Argentina and had joined our team.

Reciting my memorized phrases to a middle-aged lady at the very first door was bittersweet. I was happy that she understood my Spanish, but when she began pouring out her heart to me, I understood not one word. I thought, *Dear lady, you think I understand Spanish and I don't—just my phrases.* My redheaded partner, Molly, from Wheaton College, knew even less Spanish than I. But one of our phrases said, *We're here to learn.* At the un-Christmaslike service at church, I found myself a verse to memorize—my first in Spanish—"Porque por fe andamos, no por vista" (2 Cor. 5:7). Short and to the point. "For we walk by faith, not by sight." Whenever I see that verse, I'm transported back to one tiny church, a shelter with a mere roof, much like in the manger scenes of Monterrey my first Christmas in Mexico.

While I was in Monterrey that Christmas, Dick was leading a team in Guadalajara. He felt a little uncomfortable as leader, since he was younger in the Lord, although age-wise older than the others. On that team were people like Dale Rhoton, who had memorized most of the New Testament, and Lud Golz, who was a man of prayer and the Word, plus several others whom Dick felt should have been leading instead of him. They pulled into the city in the two-and-a-half-ton truck, ten or more of them, with all their literature and books.

Guadalajara, where the cardinal lived, was the center of fanaticism in Mexico and noted for accepting nothing without the imprimatur of the Roman Catholic Church. Catholicism in Mexico is somewhat different from that in the U. S. and other Western nations. Mexico has its patron saint, the Virgin of Guadalupe, and her image is worshiped in all of Mexico. During that Christmas, the team encountered not only worship of the Virgin of Guadalupe but of the Virgin of Zapopan as well. The main tract they distributed asked in Spanish, *"Who Has the Truth? The Catholics or the Protestants? The Bible Has the Answer!"* The verses were quoted from the Catholic Bible. Many rejected it, but thousands responded by writing in for a free Bible correspondence course in the Gospel of John—and many became believers through studying this course.

Dick wrote, "I don't know how we had the boldness on Christmas Day to park in front of the big downtown Cathedral and give out tracts and offer the little red *Evangelio de San Juan*. At first the people showed no interest, but suddenly a man got up and began preaching against us, warning people not to receive any of the literature. Amazingly, the more he spoke against us, the more the people pressed forward to see what it was all about. We asked for a small donation of twenty centavos. That way the Gospel of John would be valued and read. In a remarkably short time over seven hundred had gone out!" But afterward opposition arose. Newspaper headlines warned the populace not to receive the *propaganda protestante*. Titles and photos of the forbidden tracts and booklets were emblazoned across the front pages. Doors began to slam in their faces, and people reacted aggressively. Dick and his team were on the verge of discouragement.

However, a young friar in the Roman Catholic Church, Fortunato Cordero, was among those who had purchased a Gospel that Christmas Day. During our orientation sessions back at Moody, we had been challenged to believe the Lord for a faithful person in Mexico who would continue on after we left. Fortunato would turn out to be Dick's faithful man. The very next day Fortunato returned, seeking, and Dick prayed with him to receive Christ into his life. Afterward, a missionary named Robert Brown, who worked with converted priests, began discipling and training him.

Fortunato became a powerful evangelist, taking the gospel to all the mountain regions around Guadalajara.

During the last few days in Guadalajara, several of the team were attacked with stones, and their books and tracts were confiscated to be burned; but later they were encouraged to hear that the man in charge of the book burning kept back one copy of each title for himself. The night before they left, Dick was still giving out tracts when three guys suddenly pinned him to a wall and said, "We told you to leave! If you don't leave soon, you might not leave here alive!"

They also demanded he hand over what literature he had left. Dick had been trained in the military in self-defense and was tempted in that moment, with one guy in front of him and one on each side, to let his "old nature" respond. Something in him said, *Give a swift kick to the middle one with your knee, while using both arms to smash the ones on either side!* But at that moment the verse in 2 Timothy 2:24 (KJV) came to him: "The servant of God must not strive but be gentle unto all men." So he surrendered his tracts and booklets. The team left the next day—the day they had scheduled to leave—greatly relieved that it was time to go, and thankful to God for His protection as children pelted them with small stones on their way out of the city.

On returning to Moody, everyone buckled down for end-of-semester exams. George Verwer graduated, and he and Drena got married in Gary, Indiana. Dick and I, along with other members of the team, attended the wedding. George and Drena left straightway for

Mexico to begin Spanish studies at the university in preparation for getting the gospel into Spain, a very closed country under Franco. George left Dick in charge of continuing the prayer meetings, recruiting and training the students for the next summer's outreach, and leading them down to Mexico. After graduation Dick would move to Mexico City to oversee the work together with Baldemar Aguilar, the national director who lived in Monterrey.

My father and my fiance meet. Dick is wearing his dad's brown wool coat.

During semester break Dick went with me to Palmyra, Illinois, to meet my family. Later during spring break, we caught a ride to Greenville, Mississippi, with the Selfs, a couple from Mississippi, in order for Dick to introduce me to his family. We caught a train back north for the last half of his last semester.

Dick's part-time job in the post office putting up mail for evening school students helped pay his expenses. Mainerd Tom, part of the Mexico group, also worked there, so they made a good team. At times I would go down to check my mail, and I liked to say, "I've come down to cheer you up." Dick claimed that my coming always cheered him up. One evening I went down to find a package from home. Happy event! I always encouraged my mother and two sisters to make cookies or fudge and send because all the girls would come flocking to my room. On this night I received a box of fudge and shared some with Dick and Mainerd. But the following day I got bad news: the fudge had thrown Mainerd into sick bay. We did not know the fudge contained peanut butter or that he was allergic to peanuts!

Dick and I saw each other briefly in Monterrey that hot summer, where I was working with a girls' team. My team leader, Jean Hall (now Davey) gave us permission to go for a hike up Saddle Mountain overshadowing Monterrey. It was a memorable outing—we got caught in a sudden downpour and ran for refuge to the porch of a nearby building, where guards pointed their rifles at us, saying we were trespassing, and threatened to shoot. We begged their pardon, telling them we were just out for a walk up the mountain and weren't aware we were on private property.

Jean named me treasurer for the girls' team in Monterrey that summer. We saved every *centavo* we could to send to Dick in Mexico City. We knew he had some big book bills to cover, so we limited ourselves to one *peso* (eight cents US) each for lunch each day. With my *peso* I would get a banana, a small Coke and a piece of bread. We stayed out six to eight hours each day, going door to door in the hot, dry heat of Monterrey. Sometimes people would invite us in for lemonade and a respite from sun. We took salt tablets to prevent dehydration. Jean taught me how to bargain at the downtown market and sent me each Saturday with the team's shopping list. "Never accept the first price they give you," she said. "They expect you to talk them down." I found if I offered half the price they quoted, we would bargain until we eventually met halfway, with my paying 75 percent of the original asking price.

That's the summer I learned Spanish. I basically must have learned it as a child learns to speak. I'd hear certain words over and over, and by the end of the day sounds would be spinning around in my head. "Aha!" moments would come when words joined together with their meanings. *Ahorita no* was the first one: "Not right now." Then followed, *No tengo dinero* and *No tengo tiempo*: "I don't have money" and "I don't have time." I didn't like the depressive, *No quiero nada*: "I don't want anything," or *No me interesa*: "I'm not interested." One day I shocked a girl by responding, *Si, le interesa!* "Yes, you are interested!" I always abhorred indifference. I was blown away the first time a lady said to me, *Mi casa es tu casa:* "My house is your house." I could actually come and live in her house, I thought! Never had I received such an offer of hospitality! After hearing it multiple times, however, I realized it was a formality; but I did feel so welcomed and accepted in this country I would be making my home.

My second Christmas campaign was mainly helping Dick. He lived in the back of *Vida Abundante,* our bookstore on Mexico City's Independencia Avenue, which had been opened by George Verwer the Christmas before. Edmundo Ricoy from Spain, with his wife and daughter, welcomed me into their home, and Dick escorted me there every evening when the campaign activities were over. On Christmas Day he said, "I have a surprise!" It was hot roasted chicken and freshly made potato chips for a picnic on the green grass under the trees at Chapultepec Park. What a treat! I had again fled Chicago's snowy winter and could hardly believe this city's sunshiny warmth. Mexico City with its altitude of 7,250 feet enjoys a mild climate all year round, and the trees and grass are always green.

* * *

Chapter 2

The 1960s
Marriage and Motherhood in Mexico

Dick was in the middle of his first full year heading up the work in Mexico, along with Baldemar, and I was halfway through my senior year at Moody Bible Institute, planning our June wedding in my spare moments.

That last year at Moody, I had Dr. Mercer in Advanced Theology. He had come fresh out of Dallas Theological Seminary with ultra-Calvinistic views. According to his view of the scriptures, God had not only predestined all those who were to be saved but also had chosen those who were to be lost; and it was totally by His will and design. We had nothing whatsoever to do with it. I remember standing on the street corner waiting to catch my bus to Cook County Hospital for one of my weekly practical Christian work assignments. *What am I doing here?*

Why should I go talk to sick people about salvation if their destinies are already predetermined? Isn't it pointless in that case to be going?

Dr. Alfred Martin, my professor in Daniel and Revelation, must have known what some of us were experiencing, because one day I entered his class to hear him say, "I like to imagine it this way. Arriving at the portals of heaven, I see these words emblazoned over the gate: *Whosoever will may come.* As I walk through, I turn around to see inscribed on the inside of the gate: *Chosen in Him before the foundation of the world.*"

At another time, teaching from Daniel chapter 9, Dr. Martin told about Daniel finding Jeremiah's prophecy of seventy years of Babylonian captivity determined upon the Jewish nation. Calculating the times given, Daniel saw that the seventy years were due to be up, and he began to pray for God to do what He had said He would do and restore the people to their land. In prayer and confession of sin for himself and all the people, Daniel actively entered in with God in seeing His will done. "O Lord, hear, O Lord, forgive, O Lord, hearken and do!" *I will not passively stand by but actively collaborate with God to see His will accomplished.*

Another item helped me significantly that year. A speaker for the annual Founder's Week Conference in February chose as his theme, "When the Lord Comes to His Temple," based on the verse from Zechariah, "And the Lord, whom ye seek, shall suddenly come to His temple." Each day that week he told a story of Jesus actually coming into the temple in Jerusalem, and the results. The day that spoke to my need was, "When Jesus comes to His temple, there will be no more questions." This is not because they are tossed out or unimportant but because they are answered with sublime wisdom that causes the inquirers to marvel. There in the temple Jesus answered the Pharisees with such wisdom that their questions ceased.

Dr. Mercer didn't agree with about half of what I'd written on the final exam paper and made it known in red ink. With each question he asked, I gave back exactly what he had taught and what I knew he *expected* us to answer—but along with each I put, "But the Bible *also* says ..." listing other Scriptures with their corresponding references. I wanted to be submissive, but in my upbringing in Bible-believing churches that held opposing views on a number of issues, I had tentatively concluded that in God's mind they must not be incompatible since both are written in His Holy Scriptures. Could there be some things our minds are not yet equipped to understand but one day will?

We had asked Rev. Parker to marry us. However, in my youthful inexperience I did not realize how much this meant to him and his wife and made one of the worst mistakes of my life. On a weekend not long before the wedding I was home and happened to be shopping at Kate's Grocery. As I reached the end of an aisle, the new pastor suddenly appeared and blocked my way with his cart. "This is not right," he said, "that you have invited a former pastor to return and do your wedding." I was stunned. I hadn't realized it was out of order. "Since I've been here everyone has invited a former pastor, and no one has ever invited me."

"I didn't realize I had done wrong in inviting him," I conceded. "I'll let Brother Parker know it's necessary to change it. I'm sure he'll understand." Did I hear a happy whistling as he turned and sailed out of the store?

I asked Thelma, my maid of honor, to please let the Parkers know what had happened. "They were very disappointed," she said. "They had already told all their friends about the wedding. He wonders if the two pastors couldn't each have a part."

"No, that wouldn't work," I said, relaying the message back to them

They were crushed. They were demolished. They were shamed and would not even come to the wedding. They had been true friends and mentors, and I lost them in one fell swoop. It would take years to regain the trust and closeness we once had.

Dick's family came from Mississippi up to Illinois for the wedding: his mother, his sister Mary Ellen, and his brothers, Davis and Billy. My grandparents came up from Arkansas, but my Grandpa Smith doesn't appear in any of the photographs. He was not used to wearing a suit and hurried over to the house to get back into his overalls! We invited an MBI classmate, Jim McKelvey, down from Chicago to sing for us, "I'd Rather Have Jesus" and "The Lord is

Our Shepherd." At the reception he sang "Anywhere with Jesus We Can Safely Go." I asked my mother why she was crying, and she said, "Because you're going so far away," and then she added, "and Dick probably won't even get you a washing machine." Both things were true, of course, but I consoled her that Mexico wasn't terribly far away and she needn't worry about the washing machine.

Down the church steps with rice pelting us.
Wedding Day June 24, 1961

Dick wanted to carry me over the threshold of our new home in Mexico City and let me climb a ladder up into the loft where we would sleep. "Honey, I can't live here," I said. It was the tiny Mina bookstore, one of the branches off the main store. Our policy was not to spend money on ourselves, but this would not do. There was barely room to turn around. He told Ignacio Gonzalez, our manager in the main store, and Mr.Gonzalez agreed. He put us in a nearby hotel room for three nights while he and Dick searched for suitable housing. A newspaper ad offered us a one-bedroom apartment in the Colonia Portales in the south of the city. The cable car passing in front of our main bookstore also ran within a block of the apartment house. It was on the second floor, clean and freshly painted in pale yellow and my neighbor Emma across the hall became my friend. A bed was all we had to buy. The bookstore supplied us with a long green shelf to put our things in, a table, two chairs, a wardrobe in which to hang our clothes, and a hot plate. We signed a one-year contract for three hundred pesos ($24 dollars) a month rent for our little piece of heaven on earth.

Each morning before going downtown to the bookstore, we would grab our book bags and go door to door in our neighborhood to witness and distribute literature. With the proceeds from any sales, we were able to buy our fruit, vegetables, and eggs and pay our fare of .35 *centavos* each on the *tranvia*. Dick and I did everything together. That first summer we traveled around in Loretta Streich's car, which she loaned to us, visiting the summer teams working in Monclova and other cities, fellowshipping with them and seeing what their needs were for literature, etc. We also visited the bookstores in different cities to encourage the workers and see how each store was doing.

When the loaned car went back with its owner, Loretta Streich, to the States at the end of the summer campaign, we began to travel by bus with Carmen Davila, director of the Methodist Deaconess School, to mountain villages in the state of Puebla, to take books and help with conferences.
 I was never so scared in my life as on those high, winding highways, where the bus clung to the mountain's edge, threatening to drop off into the unseen as the daring driver passed on blind curves. At night it was even scarier whenever a driver would turn off his headlights before entering a curve.
 "Why do you cut off your lights?" Dick asked.
 "So I can see the beams of the other vehicle if one is coming," the driver answered.
 "But what if he has the same idea and cuts off his lights, too?" Dick said
 Don't even ask.
 Anticipating our next trip to Puebla, I prayed, "Lord, please give me victory over this fear." As I waited, I felt the Lord impressing me to consider the worst thing that could happen. I thought of dying as probably the worst—or being left a widow or an invalid. Then I remembered a life verse I had adopted two summers before when teaching the book

of Philippians to my cabin of teenage girls at New England Keswick: "For to me to live is Christ, and to die is gain." Every time after that as my foot touched the bottom rung of one of those *Flecha Roja* buses, I would say, "Lord, You are with me no matter what, and if this is your time for me to go, I am ready." My heart was kept in perfect peace.

Christmas of 1961, I was a bride of six months standing in front of Mexico City's Balderas Methodist Church, welcoming the cars containing fifty-six students who'd driven the thirty-six hours straight through from Chicago—just as we'd done in years past. These evangelistic campaigns would be a central feature of our lives for the next few decades. Yvonne Fittz stood there on the sidewalk with the group from Wheaton College, travel-weary and wide-eyed but eager to get started. "Am I going to be a group leader?" she asked. "I was a leader at Wheaton." This was my first year alongside Dick putting zealous college-age, short-term missionaries to work in their foreign host country. Yvonne was a great leader, and still is, together with her husband Roger Malstead.

Mother sent down a small package with the car from Moody, and I almost panicked when I left it on a pew inside Balderas Church and later went for it and it wasn't there. But it showed up. There was fudge and a fruitcake, a Papermate pen for Dick, and nylons and cologne for me. I couldn't have been happier, just having a taste of "home."

My diary pages from Mark's birth:

May 10, 1962. Thursday. This is the day the doctor calculated the baby would come. It's Mother's Day in Mexico, and two ladies in particular sit with me at length in our tiny quarters in the back of the bookstore. One is Mrs. Gonzalez. She tells me how her first baby was a month late. "First babies often are," she says. Wow, that's not very encouraging! Later when the other lady comes to visit me, she bears the same bad tidings—her first baby also was nearly a month late. First babies being a month late is news to me. But the day passes by as always and nothing happens.

That evening as Dick and I step off the streetcar near our apartment in Portales, I'm feeling pretty low. I happen to look down at my feet and notice that my ankles are swollen. Oh, no! How horrible! My baby hasn't come today, and now my ankles have swelled, and what if he's a month late and I have to go a whole month with swollen ankles! Dick tries to console me, but I fall asleep that night with my emotions at an all-time low, while attempting to resign myself to another month of waiting atop swollen ankles.

May 11, 1962, Friday, 2:30 a.m. (about four hours later), I'm awakened by my first labor pain. I lie still, though, and check the clock to make sure. They've got to be regular to be the real thing.

4:00 a.m. Yes, the contractions are regular—thirty minutes apart—so I awaken Dick. He's in a dither of excitement, ready to rush me out the apartment door immediately. I beg for time, knowing the pains are plenty far enough apart still. This is wonderful! My baby isn't late after all—in fact, he's right on time, because this is the exact day nine months ago Dick and I figured I had conceived—August 11, 1961, in Zacapauxtla, one of the small mountain villages in Puebla.

6:00 a.m. We're sitting meekly on a polished wooden bench in the entrance to the hospital, Sanatorio Lourdes, where arrangements had been made some months before. We reported in at the desk on our arrival and then found ourselves this seat. Suddenly someone snaps awake, realizing I'm in labor, and apologetically whisks me up to my room. My doctor, Alfonso Mejia Corona, arrives and checks my dilation. The nurses prepare me for delivery and then leave Dick and me alone in the room together.

9:00 a.m. Dick is sitting in a little chair beside my bed, holding my hand, encouraging me. The pains are about five minutes apart. Suddenly, the bed starts shaking. Since he's the only one in the room with me, I say, "Honey, please don't shake the bed."

"But I'm not shaking the bed," he replies, puzzled.

We look out at the hospital wing visible through our window. The whole building is swaying, and we realize it's an earthquake! So I like to say Mark's birth was an earthshaking event!

9:45 a.m. They wheel me to the delivery room. Dick must stay in the waiting room. The doctor sits with me the whole time. I have told him, "I want nothing for the pain. I want to be awake when the baby is born." So I'm surprised when after about an hour an anesthesiologist suddenly clamps a mask over my face. I feel myself floating away and start flailing my arms trying to fight off the loss of control. But instead, I hear myself laughing in the distance as I lose consciousness.

12:53 p.m. Mark is born—a perfect, healthy, beautiful baby boy—although I'm not aware of the glorious moment till a couple of hours later. Whatever they gave me really put me out.

3:15 p.m. I wake up back in my room, feeling wonderfully rested. I grab my stomach. How marvelous! The baby is born! I turn to my left and see a pink piggy bank on a little table by the wall. Oh, my! That must mean I've got a girl. Everything is so quiet. I get up, wrap my gown shut, and go out into the hallway, looking for Dick or my doctor. A couple of nurses are standing there. I ask them if the pink piggy bank means I have a girl, and they say yes. I ask them if my husband or Dr. Corona is around, and they say they'll check.

I crawl back into bed, feeling so good. Can this be what it's like to have a baby? I've never felt better in my life. I wait a while and nothing happens, so I get up again, put on my housecoat and slippers and go back out into the hall. The same nurses are there, and I ask them if I can please see my baby. Another nurse suddenly appears with authoritative stride and chews out the two younger ones. "What do you mean by letting her get out of bed! Don't you know she just gave birth this noon?" They put me back to bed and show me a button I'm supposed to turn on if I want assistance.

Then they bring a little bundle of love and place him in my arms, ushering in one of the happiest moments of my life. He's beautiful! Absolutely beautiful! As I lift the blanket, I see a miniature version of Dick in the little newborn face. The nurses are crazy about him and make like they don't want to leave him with me, but I insist! They show me how to nurse him—and he already knows how. I want to go home right then with my husband and my baby, but of course that's impossible; so I resign myself to stay put and let them wait on me hand and foot. May as well enjoy it while it lasts.

Two days later, Sunday 10:00 a.m. We check out of the hospital and arrive back in our little apartment. Dick is a wonderful housekeeper—cooking, doing dishes, everything! My neighbor, Emma, in the apartment in front of ours insists that she will do all the diapers plus my shopping. "We're here to help one another," she says. I've had two other women offer to do the diapers, too. It's the custom here that the woman not do anything for forty days after the baby is born. All her internal organs need to regain and retain their proper position, they say. I don't believe in that, and Emma says she doesn't entirely either, but she thinks I should not do anything for at least eight days. She scolds me on Monday when I have already washed the diapers and left them for her to carry up to the roof to hang out to dry. Okay, I give.

Mark is such a good baby. He only cries when he's hungry—with his little fist in his mouth! I can count on it being every two and a half to three hours, but I wish it would be more often because I've got so much milk. On his fourth day, Beverly Burke, a former classmate from Moody who serves with the Harvesters and lives nearby, comes over and takes a couple of pictures. I am so glad, because we don't have a camera. I can't remember what I'm busying myself with later, but Dick is lying on the bed next to Mark for about forty-five minutes, just *looking* at him. Finally, he speaks, without moving his gaze away: "He's nice." *Welcome, Mark Odell Griffin to our family.*

It's Friday. Mark is one week old today. Dick has gone to the bookstore, and Mark and I are alone in the apartment. All of a sudden everything starts to shake. It's another earthquake. Dogs howl, children scream, mothers shout—a cacophony of noise there in the apartments. I'm quiet though, praying, and protecting my little son. No damage is done. It gives me quite a scare, though, and I have a few nightmares after that about earthquakes and falling from windows of tall buildings.

After experiencing a few more tremors, however, my mind is at rest, and the nightmares stop. I can see the quakes have a certain pattern and duration and don't do significant damage. When I'm downtown I like to stand with the bookstore workers out on the sidewalk and watch with intrigue the movements of the earthquake-proof Latin American Tower, the tallest building in Latin America, with its built-in sway factor of seven meters.

For Christmas 1962 in Mexico City, I had a studio picture taken of seven-month-old Mark and sent it out with our Christmas cards. Eighty students came down from five schools: Moody, Wheaton, Emmaus, Greenville College, and Taylor University. A small package arrived in one of the cars from Moody on Christmas Eve. With excitement I put up a tiny tree on a small table and placed the gifts from home around the tree to open the next morning. There was a shirt for Dick, Cashmere Bouquet and a slip for me, and a little blue rattle and teething toys for Mark. The package also had cookies, candy, and nuts—what a treat! Karen Peterson from Milwaukee was living with us that year, and she gave me a bottle of Avon perfume. Dave and Sandy App invited us for Christmas Eve, and we all stepped next door for a piñata party. Such emotion whacking that piñata! Mark screamed in fright every time the children screamed in delight, and we had to make it a short night!

The Ingrams from England invited us Christmas Day, and I was seated in the place of honor at Mr. Ingram's right so Mark could easily tip over the distinguished host's lemonade, even breaking the glass. Mrs. Ingram hadn't gotten the turkey into the oven soon enough, so it wasn't quite done. The high altitude of Mexico City makes some things take hours longer to cook.

Everybody probably remembers where he or she was on November 22, 1963, when the news came. I was standing in my kitchen on the second floor we'd had built in the back of the bookstore. I heard

Mr. Gonzalez plodding up the wooden staircase. I glanced down at my greatly extended waistline, nine months pregnant minus one week. "President Kennedy has been assassinated," he said, stricken. The nation was shocked. The world was shocked. We grieved. Mexico grieved.

Eight days later, amid the Saturday afternoon bustle in the bookstore, I said to Dick, "My labor pains have started. But it'll be a while yet, so let's not hurry. Let's just get on the streetcar here in front of the store. We've got plenty of time."

"No! The second baby comes faster!" he said, already hailing a taxi. I grabbed my bag and climbed in as he gave instructions to the driver: *"Sanatorio Lourdes!"*

Dr. Corona met us there, got me prepped for the delivery room, and said, "You take a long time, so I'm going out for a cup of coffee."

The baby had his own schedule, though, and before anybody else was ready, he was!

"Where's her doctor? Where's her doctor?" all the nurses were dashing about screaming. Someone fished him out of the coffee shop, just as little Steve began to appear!

They gave me something again, and when I had barely begun to regain consciousness back in the room, I saw Dick standing at the end of the bed with an enormous grin. "We've got another boy!" he said.

"Another boy?" I asked, musingly.

"Yes, another boy," he repeated, still grinning.

"Another boy?" I asked again, still trying to grasp the news in my semi-alert stage.

"Yes, another boy," he said again, patiently, smiling quizzically.

I had made pink clothes, thinking we would have a girl. That's how it was in my family—first my brother, then me. Later on, realizing it's the man who determines the sex of a child, and studying Dick's family tree, I accepted that we would have only boys—and we rejoice to see God's perfect plan in that. *Welcome, Steven Richard Griffin, to our family.*

Since I'd given birth to Steve on November 30, I didn't get involved in the Christmas campaign as I normally did. I took Stevie and Mark out to the Presbyterian Seminary one day, though, to meet the students and play in the sun.

My little Christmas tree sat forlorn that Christmas morning. I had cried Christmas Eve with homesickness on learning that the Moody students' bus had broken down in Kansas City with our small, "Do not open until Christmas" box from home on board and would not be coming down. One of the cars from Georgia had an accident on the ice in Mississippi and didn't make it either—one broken back and one broken collarbone. That was worse.

Christmas morning Dick looked at the little tree and said, "You didn't get your package. When are you taking the tree down?" I told him I was leaving it up till the presents came. Dick's mother sent ten dollars for the boys, so I got them some gifts and some hankies for Dick.

When Dick and I arrived at the bookstore as a married couple, I remember three specific prayers we prayed together from the very beginning:

- That God would raise up Mexican youth to go out with our teams in evangelism.
- That God would raise up Mexicans to go to all parts of the world with the gospel.
- That God would provide their support through the Mexican churches.

God had begun to answer the first one. A young man named Raul Galvez who taught English in the university observed the teams in action at his Brethren church in Tacubaya. The students were inviting people in off the streets to come into the meeting, and Raul's church was packed for the first time. "Look at how they're doing that!" he said. "They hardly speak any Spanish, and they've filled our church with new people. We should be doing that!" And he began. Raul was also among the first group of Mexicans to go to Spain. Here is a snapshot of that group in front of the bookstore.

To Spain summer of 1964. **Emma Olga Aguilar, Raul Galvez, Isaias Medel, Marcelino Ortiz, Judith & Pepe Barrios.**

Christmas of 1964 in Nuevo Laredo was one of my all-time favorite Christmas campaigns. Mark was two and a half and Steve one year old. We slept on some cots in a small room off the main sanctuary of our host church, *La Iglesia Presbiteriana*. I had prayed that there would be a Christmas tree the boys could enjoy. Would you believe it? One door of our room opened into the sanctuary, and there it stood: a magnificent tree fully decorated and a joy to behold. I did the cooking for the team of guys living in that same church and was especially blessed by the life of one of them, Steven Richards. He taught us the hymn "It Passeth Knowledge That Dear Love of Thine," and he even gave me his little pocket hymnal with all the words. I treasured it. Our little Steve learned to love hymns also, and I later gave it to him—fitting, from Steven Richards to our Steven Richard.

Our fledgling missionary evangelistic organization, originally called "Send the Light" came to be known as "Operation Mobilization" the summer before in France when George Verwer got the vision to mobilize students in Europe to use their vacation times for outreach. Our men's team, too, in Mexico, in keeping with this same dynamic street-corner spirit, invited men in off the street that evening to eat with us and present to them the good news, the gospel of Jesus Christ. To everyone's astonishment, little Mark suddenly stood up in his place at the table and began to sing these words in Spanish, clearly without missing a beat. God was in that!

> *Solo el poder de Dios puede cambiar tu ser.*
> *La prueba yo te doy, él me ha cambiado a mí.*
> *¿No ves que soy felíz sirviendo al Señor?*
> *Nueva criatura soy, nueva soy.*

Translation:

> *Only the power of God can change your life.*
> *I give you proof, He has changed me.*
> *Don't you see how happy I am serving the Lord?*
> *I am a new creature, I am new.*

What a powerful message it was from the lips of a young child. Jesus said in Matthew 21:16 that out of the mouths of babes God had perfected praise. *Will we perhaps see some of those men in heaven partly because of Mark's song that evening?*

Steve crawled down off his cot one night and up onto ours, which wasn't built to hold three of us. We all came crashing to the floor. Steve screamed with fright, but no one was hurt, and the eighteen guys sleeping in the other rooms didn't wake up. One afternoon Mark ventured too close to the red-ant beds while playing out in the churchyard. They covered his tender flesh and bit him all over, leaving huge white whelps. His commentary on the campaign: "The ants bit me."

In contrast, Christmas of 1965 in Monterrey found me rushing all day long, doing the cooking for a team of fellows like the previous year, only the setting was not so peaceful. We were in the headquarters church, and every team that was arriving, leaving, or passing through ate with our team of twenty-five at a moment's notice—or no notice at all. It was fun, though, because they were ravenous and grateful for the food. A Christmas package arrived on December 22 with a lovely dress for me and a neat sweater for Dick, which he wore all day every day for the rest of the campaign. Stevie liked his bother Mark's little wind-up train much better than his furry kitten, and they fought over it. "Mine? Mine?" Stevie would ask. Our little family was set up in the nursery of the large *Iglesia Metodista* with all the cribs at our disposal and our own bathrooms.

In Operation Mobilization we were constantly on the go. Dick would be invited to preach in a different church just about every Sunday, and I dutifully accompanied him. As our little family grew, baby and diaper bag came along with me, too. We got acquainted with churches all over Mexico City and other cities and villages of the Mexican Republic.

One day Dick said to me, "Mark and Steve are old enough to go into their own Sunday school class now. They should have a regular one."

"How can we do that?" I asked.

"You should choose a church you like and take the boys there every Sunday. I'll keep going all the places I'm invited." So the boys and I began boarding a northbound bus every Sunday morning heading up the busy *Avenida Insurgentes Norte*. There was a field of clover where we disembarked and walked one block east to the church. My two little boys delighted in picking clover blossoms for me. They liked their teacher and their class, and I enjoyed the excellent teaching of the renowned Rene Zapata. I would muse, though, on my longing to have a part in something. *I wish they would at least invite me to be a teacher's helper with the little ones,* I thought, but they never did.

One Sunday morning something happened, though, in the boys' preschool room that frightened them. They both cried and pulled back after that and refused to go in, but were unable to tell me what was wrong. I kept trying to encourage them to go back and even invited their teacher over to talk, but we couldn't uncover the problem. I missed my class in the Gospel of Luke, but I didn't feel I should force the boys to go.

Carmen Davila, who had taken us with her into the mountain villages of Puebla, served as head of the *Escuela Metodista de Diaconisas*. She came into the bookstore one day and invited me to teach a course on the Gospel of John in Spanish to the young ladies. That Gospel is probably my favorite book in all the Bible, and that was my first experience teaching in Spanish to a beautiful group of earnest young women preparing for ministry.

First Mexico Year Team 1965-66. Apolos Andrade, Wayne & Joyce Ericksmoen, Angela Martinez, Adoracion Villegas, Marcia Williams, Jane & Dennis Renich

We had the large campaigns in major cities every Christmas, the summer teams spread out in different locations, and there was ongoing evangelistic outreach in local churches. Now the opportunity arose to have a team working for the whole year. Dennis and Jane, Wayne and Joyce, and Marcia (pictured above) all came down from Bethany Fellowship in Minneapolis. Apolos, Angela, and Adoracion were the Mexicans who joined, plus Elsa Ramirez, Felix Juarez, and his sister Paz. We rented a team house, and many people in the community came to the Lord and were meeting and studying regularly with the group. Dick looks back on this time as a missed opportunity. Wherever our OM teams worked, we had the policy of joining with the local churches in evangelistic outreach. We discipled new believers but depended on local churches in the area to receive them in as members and see to their continued nurture and growth. In this case the churches in the area, because of internal problems, were not able, and many of the new believers fell away. Dick often felt saddened that he did not continue meeting with them to see the group grow into a congregation.

The summer of 1966 my sister Linda married and invited me to be matron of honor in her wedding. She wondered if four-year-old Mark could be the ring bearer. When I talked to Mark about it he happily agreed. When I asked him if he thought Stevie could be a ring bearer, he said, "No, he can't carry it. It's too heavy."

Dennis and Jane had to make a trip back to the States that summer, and there was room in their van for the two boys and me. Dick reluctantly conceded, feeling some reservation because of the condition of Dennis's vehicle. He committed us to the Lord, though, and was in prayer for us as we traveled. I was in prayer too, singing and meditating the whole morning on Psalm 27: "The Lord is my light and my salvation; whom then shall I fear? The Lord is the strength of my life; of whom then shall I be afraid?" I had my brother Alton's Bible, which I had borrowed from him and was returning, and I was meditating from it.

I also pondered with some satisfaction the $40 that I had saved in the bank over a period of time in a small savings account for Mark and Steve, money that had been given to them. I had it in my purse, and in the States we would be able to buy things we could not get in Mexico. I also had a five-gallon tin of pure honey for my dad. He was going to love that! Before reaching San Luis Potosi, Dennis pulled over and asked if I would like to drive a while. Of course, I would. I enjoyed driving and had formerly been one of the assigned drivers on these trips. I was not acquainted with Dennis's van, however. He cautioned me about the play in the steering wheel. Wow, this was strange to drive with, especially on this large vehicle. But we were making it fine along the long lonely barren desert highway of northern Mexico, and Dennis dozed off behind me on the seat with Mark and Steve.

We were approaching a place where you go up and over a small hill. As we cleared the top of it, I saw a Volkswagen Bug putt-putting along up ahead. I decided to pass him, seeing no other traffic around. But as I started to pull out, I noticed in my rearview mirror a car just clearing the hill was pulling out to pass me. I decided to turn my steering wheel back and stay behind the VW and lightly tapped the break. Under normal circumstances I would not even have remembered these moves, but the play in the wheel must have caused the van to behave as though it had hit a patch of slick ice. We sailed off the road to the right, then across the highway to the left, where we rolled over in the ditch on the far side. No one was hurt. Praise God! The highway patrol took us on in to San Luis Potosi, where Dennis and Jane caught a plane to Minneapolis. I had to use the precious, hoarded $40 for bus tickets to get the boys and me to St. Louis, where my brother Jim picked us up. He had quite a time lugging that five-gallon tin of honey, but he did it! I was sorry I never saw my brother Alton's Bible again.

For Linda's wedding my mother made my dress of forest green satin, and Joyce's too. We had just finished getting dressed the day of the wedding, when little Stevie, age two and a half, came running in from the kitchen having just eaten a bowl of beans. "Mommmmmmy!" he squealed with delight, reaching out his little arms and grabbing my satin skirt. You can see in Linda's wedding pictures the stain that remained where we tried to remove the bean juice. A unique design! Mark was supposed to escort the little flower girl, but she refused to join the procession, being made to stay up late for rehearsal the night before and awakened early for the hairdresser. She was a lovely sleeping beauty when the moment came, and Mark was a valiant young ring bearer marching alone down the aisle.

When the school year began back in Mexico in 1966, Mark started kindergarten at the *Instituto Americano Concordia*, a primary school established by the Lutherans. While in the process of enrolling him, one day I said, "Mark, would you like to go to kindergarten?"

"No, I don't want to go to kindergarten *yet*," he said. "They might ask me to make an *S*, and I don't know how to make an S." When the school year began, though, he was filled with excitement. As he learned the alphabet in Spanish and began to read, I coached him also in English. We went together to the American bookstore downtown and bought the *Dick and Jane* readers, which I had learned from. I did the same thing the following year with Steve. It was fun being a "schoolteacher" with my own children.

Christmas cards bring Christmas cheer to me. On December 20, 1966, in Mexico City, I had my little tree set up and the cards we'd received decorating the walls. With OM policy not to spend money, we didn't do presents unless the boys' grandparents sent something. The Andersons, who ran Stephanus House for missionaries, made a border trip, and I had

Mother send her Christmas package for us to our friends, the Brumbaughs, who lived at the border for the Andersons to bring back.

When we knew the Andersons had returned, the two boys and I with excitement boarded a local bus over to the center to pick up our package. "It got left in the back of the truck going on to Veracruz," Lorna Anderson said. Mark and Steve stood there like two little soldiers. The words hadn't penetrated their understanding, but they exploded like a bombshell on me. "Missionary children just have to get used to this kind of thing and accept it," she pontificated matter-of-factly. "It's part of their life, and they have to learn."

I was speechless. I was crushed. I wanted to say, "It's not the children who are having a problem with this. It's me!"

The campaign was quiet that Christmas. No students came down from the States because OM had a leadership conference in Pittsburgh. Arturo Arana, however, and his wife Hilda came up from Bolivia. The thirteen girls and two guys living with us that year had special meetings with the Bolivian evangelist. Into the quiet of that Christmas stepped Maria Vilchis, a lady my mother's age, who for four years had been my friend. She loved us and knitted sweaters for my boys and me. But whenever I wanted to talk to her about the Lord or mentioned the Bible, she would immediately change the subject. Paul and Jean White, who had worked with OM had made the initial contact with her those four years back and left her with me for follow-up. But I said to Dick once, "I'm ready to give up on Mary Vilchis. I see no response. She only wants to be my friend and practice English. Spiritually she is not open at all." How wrong I was. In the stillness of that Christmas, she became a believer at the preaching of Arturo Arana, and became an unstoppable witness and powerhouse for Christ. Later her husband came to the Lord, and her son also followed.

In the springtime, the thirteen girls living with us in the second-floor apartments were filled with anticipation about our new baby's arrival. As time drew near for his appearance, they would dash up the stairs immediately after evangelism to see if the baby had come yet. They'd see my face and moan, "You're still here!"

I had miscalculated, though, and marked my calendar wrong. I thought he was due April 15. So the beginning of April the girls threw a grand baby shower. Excitement escalated after that. Dick didn't take any out-of-town commitments after April 1 just in case. He took me for my regular checkup on April 15. As I stretched out on the examining table, Dr. Corona pulled out a tape measure and laid it across my tummy. "You are only eight and a half months," he pronounced, looking at the centimeters. "You still have two more weeks to go." He was right! Philip arrived on April 28, 1967, just when he was supposed to. *Welcome to our growing family, Philip Roy Griffin!*

The team had brought back from one of their out-of-town campaigns a lady they called *Tia Maria* to do the cooking. She was a valuable help in the kitchen, but when I returned from the hospital with Philip, I heard horror stories about her terrorizing Mark and Steve. "You are never going to see the baby," she said. "I'm going to the hospital to steal him away, and you are never ever going to see him." She would torment them with words to get a reaction and work them into a near hysteria. Mark, who was always so even-tempered, even tried to kick her. The girls had to dismiss her. She promptly headed up the street to a tavern, where she got drunk and made a big scene. On being confronted, she declared she had never been a Christian anyhow, that she only said she was so the team would bring her to Mexico City with them.

Soon after that, the Isais children from the English-speaking Capital City Baptist Church called, inviting Mark and Steve to vacation Bible school. I cradled Philip in my arms and watched as his two brothers climbed happily up the stairway to their class. They loved it from day one! So after that week, we started catching a bus south on the long Avenida Insurgentes Sur to attend Sunday school. It was ideal, given that they both had begun kindergarten at the *Instituto Americano Concordia* in Spanish, that they attend a church where English was used.

We had been going only a few weeks when the Sunday school superintendent, Liz Isais, approached me. "I've noticed your lively participation in the adult class," she said. "Since the group is large, we plan to divide it. Would you consider teaching the ladies?" I could hardly believe my ears. I had longed for the tiniest bit part, and here I was handed a class of thirty women who were eager to study the Scriptures, most of them missionaries. I delved into the Word, spending at least six hours a week in preparation for my class and loving every minute of it. I taught that class of women for twelve wonderful years.

No one knows how my dad came out alive when the train crushed his car the night of December 11, 1967, as he was driving across the signal-less tracks on his way home from work at the Farmersville coal mines. The three boys and I flew up to spend Christmas with the family in Palmyra, Illinois. All my brothers and sister were there. Daddy was out of the hospital and took his nourishment through a straw because his broken jaw was wired shut for healing. One arm was in a cast. Mother baked a turkey on Christmas Day, and I still have the wishbone among my treasures.

Linda and George had married the summer of 1966 but were waiting to start a family, so Linda took delight in showering my three boys with beautiful toys and Tonka trucks, all of the best quality. I packed them together carefully and lovingly in one suitcase for the flight back to Mexico. Would you believe the second lap of our American Airlines flight was canceled and we had a whole day's layover before being transferred onto a Braniff flight. The only seats were in first class, so there I sat in the lap of luxury among businessmen with my three travel-weary little darlings.

Instead of arriving back in Mexico City at 3:30 in the afternoon, we touched down at midnight and looked in vain for our luggage. Three suitcases were eventually delivered by the airline to our apartment on Guerrero Street. But the fourth—yes, you guessed which one—never surfaced. I had to list each item with its value in order to be reimbursed. Thankfully, the boys did not waste any tears over their lost suitcase full of toys. Their concern in the weeks following was elsewhere: "Is my granddaddy's arm well? Does he have the cast off yet?"

Christmas 1968 was spent in Ciudad Juarez and Slaton, Texas. After pre-campaign meetings in Mexico City with George Verwer, we headed up to Ciudad Juarez, a thirty-six hour drive, for the Christmas campaign. Dick got the teams going, then drove his little family the 350 extra miles on up to Aunt Nova's so we could spend Christmas with her and her family. Then he caught a bus back to Ciudad Juarez.

Aunt Nova was like a second mother to me in those days when my children were little. I missed my own mother and the counsel she would have given me in childrearing, and she missed being in touch with her grandchildren as they were growing up. I kept a little diary for her of cute tidbits that I hadn't written in letters home. It was a glorious Christmas in the heart of loving family. Betty Ruth and Betty Jean (Aunt Nova's two daughters-in-law) and I went bike riding together, gave each other perms, played Yahtzee, and made trips to Lubbock, and little Vicki Jo wanted to be included in everything I did. Aunt Nova doted over my babies.

Mother sent gifts, and Linda flew down on December 28 with presents for everyone. How special it was to be with my baby sister while she was expecting their first child—little Jody Lynn was born the following March. When time was up, I packed my young ones in the car and drove the 350 miles back to Ciudad Juarez. Dick was standing out on the sidewalk watching for us. He seemed to have calculated the precise moment we would be pulling up at the host church, or maybe he had even been standing out there for some time watching and praying for the precious cargo coming back to him.

Dick and I prayed when we moved into the new apartment, just off Insurgentes Avenue, "Dear God, help us to reach this building for You." The first person we met was Leonor, our neighbor across the hall. As we walked our children home from the Concordia school, we talked. She and her husband and two children had come from Spain, and she was very open to know more about the Bible and wanted her children to learn too.

"I have a good friend who does a Bible class in Spanish for children on Saturdays," I said. "Would you like to go tomorrow?" She was eager to attend. That day at the Sandovals' house Leonor met Jesus. She prayed the simple prayer when an invitation was given for the children, and her life was transformed forever. She witnessed to everybody of the change Christ had made in her life. She did not stop speaking of Him wherever she went—all the way to school and back, all the way to the market and back, and to our entire apartment building!

When the time came for her to move away, she knocked on my door to say goodbye. It was an emotional moment for her. "Thank you for coming to this building," she said with tears. "God sent you here for me. This is what I had been searching for all my life."

I thanked God from my heart. I never told anyone, but I had experienced a great struggle in regard to moving there. First of all, it would be more rent than we had ever paid, nine hundred pesos, which was $72 dollars a month. That made me feel guilty, spending that much money on us. In the second place, it had huge windows, which I loved because they let in lots of light, but the windows had no bars or other protection. What if my beautiful two-and-a-half-year-old Philip should climb up and open the handle and fall out a third-story window? Just the thought struck me with fear. I'm glad I let God handle the guilt and the fear, and that we did move there—for Leonor.

Her children had accepted Jesus into their hearts, too, and the daughter grew up to marry a missionary. We heard the husband also came to Christ. They later moved back to Spain and I imagined Leonor, an exuberant witness, telling everyone in her path the good news she had learned in Mexico.

L to R: *Mark, Philip, Steve, March 1968. Pictures Speak Volumes.*

Diary note from April, 1969:

Philip's a character ... dances down the sidewalk when I take him out with me, smiles at people, waves goodbye! Don't know what I'd do without that sparkling little personality!

He and Mark and Steve are all three so different. Steve has just decided this week that he's not going to be a doctor in Afghanistan. He's going to play golf with his granddaddy and make lots of money. Mark says, "You're not going to earn any money that way," but Steve insists that he is.

Mark's the practical, studious, level-headed one. He hates to waste time—and anything that doesn't fit into his scheme of things is "wasting time," like getting haircuts and doing homework. He's had his picture and name on the honor roll this whole school year as the top boy in the class, but in his catalog it's "wasted time," since according to him he already knows it all. And maybe he does. His teacher this year hasn't offered any challenge, and that's a waste of time.

For Christmas 1969 we were in the border towns of Ciudad Acuña, Mexico, and Del Rio, Texas. Those two names, "Ciudad Acuña" and "Del Rio" were like music from my childhood. On our long drives down to Arkansas from Illinois, a powerful radio station XERF came across the airwaves when no other station made it through, and I can still hear the announcer lilting out the call letters and the names of those two towns. Now, to think, they were our destination for the Christmas campaign! They were not much to behold actually, just dusty little border towns. A couple days it rained, so the children who played freely all over the place had fun in the mud too. George and Drena had left Benjamin, age nine, and Daniel, age seven, in London, and brought only five-year-old Christa with them. She and the boys got along well together, and Drena and I had great times sharing.

One of the college students playfully tossed my six-year-old Stevie up in the air and somehow missed him on his way down, resulting in a small fracture on the middle finger of his right hand. Stevie didn't seem to mind the splint for two weeks, and the thought of starting back to school not having to do homework brought a grin to his face.

A shiny, brand-new refrigerator stood welcoming us back as we entered our apartment that new year. The men's Sunday school class at Capital City had it delivered just before we left on the campaign. Bye-bye to the little ice chest my brother Jim and his wife Mona had provided years ago, and to the iceman, who faithfully delivered a block of ice every day to keep our milk cold. The refrigerator certainly made life easier for me, not having to go to the market every day.

Another profound blessing that Christmas was a card and letter from my mentors, the Parkers, who had been excluded from my wedding. How wonderful to be forgiven at last for a hurt as deep as the one I inflicted unintentionally on two beautiful people I loved so dearly.

* * *

Chapter 3

The 1970s
Of Teaching and Traveling

We worked the summer of 1970 in several villages in the state of Morelos together with OM leaders Ron and Nan George and a busload of teenagers they brought down from California. One morning Dick headed out with three-year-old Philip on the back fender of a borrowed bicycle, pedaling to the next village. Philip's heel got caught in the spokes and cut open. Dick carried him—both of them in great pain—all the way back to the village of Zapata, pushing the bike along that lonely dirt road with not a soul in sight. The little village doctor had no anesthesia, but he cleaned the wound and sewed it up with many stitches while I held Philip in place on the surgical table. Philip crawled for nine days with the injured, bandaged foot held up off the floor. The day it was well and he suddenly discovered he could walk again, he burst into happy peals of laughter!

The five of us slept that summer on mats in a small corner room that faced the street. A tall light pole stood on that corner. One night during a severe thunderstorm, lightning struck the pole, and I lay trembling in Dick's arms at the impact of the deafening noise louder than I ever imagined existed.

As I lay there, I thought of my mother's fear of lightning, which her mother passed on to her. Grandma would herd her entire brood to the storm cellar, where we sat out storms. I had consciously resisted having that fear ever pass on to me. But this was too close, way too close. As the storm raged and I was still trying to calm down, I felt the Lord whisper to me, "It will never come any closer to you than that." *Thank You, blessed Ruler of the storms*

Christmas 1970 took us to Ciudad Juarez and El Paso. Dick and Steve went with the team back to the border city where we had been two years before with two hundred students. Dick brought back statistics someone had compiled: two hundred and twenty participants. The amazing thing was that forty of them were Mexican. When we first started the campaigns, there were no Mexicans at all going out with us, so this was an extraordinary answer to prayer. Twelve churches participated, over seventy-five thousand homes were visited, five hundred thousand pieces of literature were distributed, and the teams conducted twenty-five open-air services.

When Mark finished second grade and Steve first grade, their school, *Instituto Americano Concordia*, closed. What were we going to do? Some missionary friends, Max and Sinikka Doherty, recommended the *Sara Alarcon,* where their two boys, Pat and Mike, attended. But Mark and Steve had a difficult time adjusting to the new regimen and came home stressed and unhappy at the end of every day. They had longer hours, more homework, a strict military regimen, and long bus rides to and from school.

"Lord, please let their school open back up again," I would pray. "My boys are not happy where they are now. Please let their school reopen." The Lord didn't answer that prayer, though, and Mark and Steve were still enduring the difficulties when the first semester ended and it was time for Christmas break. I didn't know how to pray as I ought for their schooling, but God knew my heart and their need and did something beyond my wildest dreams. *Concordia* didn't reopen, but God opened the door to Greengates.

R-i-i-i-ng went the phone over by the window. "Helen, this is Rosina Curry. I teach at Greengates School. They're in desperate need of a teacher for the first two weeks of January in the pre-primary department. You have your working papers, don't you? Would you fill in for two weeks till they find a teacher? I'll be right next door and will help you get oriented."

"Sure! I'll be glad to," I said, taking down the information. When the two weeks were up, Mr. Coelho, the headmaster, called me into his office. "We like your work," he said. "Would you be interested in taking the job full-time? I told him about my three sons. "No problem," he replied. "You can put them in school here. We will give them a 50 percent discount this year, and next year full scholarships."

"But my youngest is only three and a half years old," I said.

"That's okay. We can put him in the pre-kinder group."

The boys took to Greengates immediately. It was God's provision for them to get high-quality education. We could never have afforded the tuition fees, but with the discounts plus my salary everything was covered; and when we later moved into the area, my salary exactly paid our house rent. The schedule was ideal. I taught from 9:00 a.m. to 12:00 noon. So Philip and I got home at noon and had the meal ready by the time Mark and Steve finished at 2:00 p.m. and caught the school bus back down the hill. "This is the nicest thing that could happen to me!" I declared.

But I learned the position had opened up because the teacher had walked out—and I could see why she had. Four unruly, disruptive boys had banded together and claimed control of the classroom. I had to reclaim it in order to teach anything, a challenging experience for me. I had walked into their domain, and it was like training a non-housebroken dog who had already marked out his territory. Dr. Dobson's book *Dare to Discipline* offered valuable advice, and Mark's third-grade teacher sold kits for making hooked rugs. I found it therapeutic on arriving home each day to work out my frustrations on that rug—which turned out to be beautiful, by the way!

In the fall of 1971 my new class of twenty-six walked into *my* territory, where boundaries were already marked. I had no serious discipline problems all the remaining years I taught at Greengates, and I was favored with being given some of the top students. *He is able to do exceedingly abundantly above all we ask or think.*

Christmas 1971, we were in Monterrey. Dick left early with the team up to Monterrey—thirteen of them in the almost-new truck that Christ Wesleyan Church in Greenville, Mississippi, provided for us. In preparation for the trip, Dick had four brand-new *Firestone* tires put on. One of them blew out on the way up, and the truck rolled over one and a half times. Miraculously there were no serious injuries, just one broken nose. When school let out, the boys and I rode up with Carl and Evelyn Knirk, OM workers in the finance department. Our family's place in that Christmas was the "Student Center," where we stayed with a team of about thirty-five guys. We helped run a "coffee house," serving cokes as an outreach in the evening hours.

My favorite memory from that Christmas was walking down our tree-lined street with my three boys and buying cream puffs at a bakery. Mother sent a check again, which didn't get through, but I got gifts for us from them, and she replaced the check later. The boys and I prepared a package for them. We recorded a tape of them singing and Steve reciting "'Twas the Night before Christmas," but the recorder's speed was off, and with disappointment we didn't include it. We all rode back with Carl and

Evelyn, and then Dick returned with Samuel Castro to Saltillo on January 10 to pick up the repaired vehicle.

Present my body? The concept of presenting my body a living sacrifice had never been easy for me. For some reason I wanted to turn and run the other way. Then the pastor at Capital City Church, Dr. Richard M. Shurtz, began to take us verse by verse through the book of Romans. It was the most amazing study I had ever done of God's plan and what it cost Him to save us. "Your salvation is free. It didn't cost you anything," he would remind us over and over, "*but it cost Him everything.*"

Verse by verse, week by week, vivid illustrations, charts on overhead projector, review upon review—he was the consummate teacher. If you missed a study, cassette recordings were available in the library—and no one wanted to miss a study. He insisted upon the very best Bible translations available and shunned the paraphrases. One evening, though, to get a swift overview of the whole epistle, I was reading Romans all the way through from *The Living Bible,* a paraphrase, as I knelt by my bed. The magnificent doxology of glory and praise to God at the end of chapter 11 glided right into verse 1 of Romans 12 without any break. After verse 1, which I'd always wanted to flee from, "Present your body a living sacrifice," I was startled with an unexpected question right there in the text: *"When you think of what He has done for you, is this too much to ask?" (TLB)*

It almost bowled me over. Everything in me that had ever resisted suddenly melted at His words, and I answered, "No, Lord, that is *not* too much to ask." My life was revolutionized in that moment. I had an incredible desire to share my faith with other teachers at Greengates, longing to win them to Christ and study the Bible with them. My prayer life came alive, and I noticed I looked forward to communion services with an eager anticipation I had not experienced before.

When school recessed for the summer, Dick said, "Why don't you take the boys up to Illinois and spend your vacation time with your parents? I have to be traveling with the OM teams all over Mexico the whole summer. My first thought was *no*. I had been witnessing to Gladys Weeks, Philip's kindergarten teacher, and she was very near to turning her life over to the Lord. *If I leave now,* I thought, *it will not be the same when I get back.*

We went, however. Dick drove us in the Valiant up to San Antonio, and he caught a bus back. I put 7,000 miles on the car that summer. When I couldn't stand to stay any longer in Sesser with my dad's escalated drinking, I would gather my three young sons like a mother hen with her chicks under her wing and take off in the Valiant to my sister's in Oklahoma or my brother's in northern Illinois.

Something else happened that summer. Mother had read a book she wanted me to read. I didn't want to, but she left it lying in plain sight on a lamp table in the living room, and the title would jump out at me every time I walked through. Unable to avoid the issue, I thought to myself, *I'll read it to please her, but I'll be able to explain it away.*

So I picked it up, *A New Song,* by Pat Boone. I didn't put much stock in celebrities, and I knew I wouldn't agree with the content, which was his personal experience with the Holy Spirit. But as I read, I realized the story was real, that he was not performing. I couldn't deny the reality of what God had done in his life. So what was I going to do then if I couldn't explain it away? I prayed, "Lord, I see that this thing You did for him is real. But I also know it is not for me. Please show me why."

Here's what came to my mind: Pat Boone had known Jesus and had gotten away, like the younger son in the parable, and had lived in the far country. When he came back destitute to the Father, a grandiose party was thrown for him. That explained it! In my case, I had never gone away as he had into the far country, so there was no need for that type of experience, which was like a big celebration. It was not until much later I saw the person I resembled in the parable. I was the older brother who stayed outside and refused to go in and be joyful with the others while the Father patiently said, "All that I have is yours, and you're welcome to it anytime you choose."

Back at Greengates School in the fall, nothing was the same. Mrs. Weeks had been dismissed from her job, and I lost contact with her. I was not the same either, as though the stress of the summer, my "copping out" on coping, and my own refusal to follow the Lord in the next step of obedience He had for me had robbed me of something precious.

After Christmas 1972 in Mexico City, I wrote Mother, "I feel like Christmas passed me by this year." Her check didn't come through for the third year in a row, and the package she sent to Lynn Stevens at Moody for the students to bring down got left at Moody. George Verwer and his son Ben, age twelve, stayed in the apartment with us, and wherever George Verwer is, there is one constant whirl of activity. My main contribution to the campaign was entertaining four lively boys in our apartment and answering the incessantly ringing phone. Dick had a bad throat and a wheezing in his chest, but refused to drop out of the action. We had 70 Mexicans, 70 Canadians, and 120 Americans participating in the outreach. Dick was happy because he was able to get George programmed on a TV station, on the radio, and in the newspapers—all practically unheard of in Mexico.

Our lives took on a new flavor when we moved into a house in the suburban district of Bulevares, north of the city near Greengates. We had an actual house, instead of a third-floor apartment over a shipping company that revved up the motors to its big trucks at 4:00 in the morning one block from the incessant traffic of the biggest avenue in the city. The boys were thrilled to trade their cement parking lot playground for a patch of grass.

One simple thing in our new house blessed me beyond belief—quietness! I could hear the clock ticking for the first time in a decade, after ten years in the very heart of Mexico City with its unrelenting, unmitigated noises. The boys loved the small front lawn with its green grass where they could toss their football, and the little back patio where they could have a pair of white rabbits, and a small alcove off the kitchen when they had parakeets.

We had four team members living with us that first year: Jim Lamb, Gonzalo Gonzalez, Daniel Bermudez, and Samuel Castro. Dick took them out every day in evangelism in our neighborhood. Whenever they made contact with an English-speaking woman who was interested in studying the Bible, they would pass her name and address to me for follow-up. After collecting quite a stack of names, I called my friend Susan Rigby. "Susan, would you like to go with me to visit English-speaking women in this area? We could invite them to do a Bible study." She liked the idea, so we called on each one and got a study going at my house.

One day in September I hopped into my Valiant to pick up a new lady who wanted to attend our study. On the way I stopped to get Elvira, age seventy-five. We were heading up a street two blocks over when suddenly a child flew out his front door and darted between parked cars right into my path. I slammed on my brakes but not in time. He sailed through the air and landed motionless about six feet in front of me. I had never been so scared in my life. I had hit a little four-year-old boy.

His mother dashed out of the house almost at his heels, grabbed him up out of the street where he lay, then jumped into the backseat of my car shouting, "Take me to the Red Cross!" Then she screamed, "He's not breathing!"

"Put your mouth on his and breathe into him," I said. She did that and got him breathing again while a crowd of neighbors converged as though drawn by a magnet.

"Take me to the Red Cross quick!" she ordered.

At that a man stepped forward and said to me, "I will take her." I got out and gave him my name, address, phone number, and license plate, as others assisted her and the child out of my car into his. "You go on back to your house," he said.

Elvira and I walked into my dining room, where several women had already arrived for the study. "You're white as a ghost!" Susan exclaimed. "What's wrong?" I could barely talk to say what had happened. I felt as white as a ghost, and the pain at having hit the child was unbelievable. Coupled with the fear for his life was the terror that the authorities were right on my heels ready to throw me into prison. That's what happened in Mexico for hitting someone.

The days that followed were painful as I waited. It hurt so bad I could not even talk about it. I did tell Liz Isais at church, and that helped. I went over to the child's house to check and found out he was in the hospital under observation for possible internal bleeding. I also discovered that the neighbor man had reported the accident to the Red Cross as a "hit and run." That way I was not incriminated, he said, because it was not my fault. At least that mountain lifted off of me. After what seemed like forever—thirteen days!—the child was finally released from the hospital. I praised God for His care over him. Surprisingly, when I went to visit the family, I was told they had moved to another city.

Christmas, 1973, was the Christmas I had longed for: having Mother and Daddy fly down to spend their holidays with us. Daddy had just retired from the coal mines in Illinois after twenty-five years, and they had moved back to Arkansas. We had been in Mexico twelve years, and it was the first time and only time they ever came.

Dick left for Torreon to lead the Christmas campaign, but the boys and I were at home to entertain my restless father, who was afraid to get into a car after his first frightening (for him) trip into downtown Mexico City, and my delighted mother, who wanted to go everywhere we went and see everything and meet everyone. The thing my dad enjoyed doing was going for a stroll down the little street of shops a couple blocks from our house, learning to use his Mexican coins and seeing if he could find somebody to converse with in English. It was colder than normal, and we had only a tiny electric heater, so it was difficult for them to keep warm. One day Daddy asked Steve if he was cold, and Steve replied, "I've been cold all my life."

During their visit I told my mother about the little boy I had hit. "Helen! That was three months ago," she said. "Why did you not tell me?"

I explained to her what it was like and how it hurt so bad I could hardly talk. I blamed myself for negligence in not foreseeing a child would actually do that. "I feel this intense anger even now," I said. "If I see a little child get anywhere near the street, I want to scream, *'What do you mean getting near the street? Streets are for cars! Get back in your house!'*" It was a comfort being able to talk to her about it. She was good at asking the right questions, and she was a good listener.

On the afternoon of September 5, 1974, Dick was washing the dishes. Standing there at the kitchen sink up to his elbows in soap suds, he suddenly called out, "I've got something in my eye!" He thought he'd splashed some suds in it, but drying it didn't help.

"Elena, can you come see what I've got in my eye?" he called out. I went and looked carefully but could see nothing.

"But there's something in there," he said, "like a butterfly." Puzzled, we drove over to the optical shop at Sears to see if they could help. They could detect nothing either.

"If it doesn't go away in a day or two, you should see a specialist," the oculist said.

So we saw a specialist. "I can't be sure," he mused, "but it looks like one of three things: a hemorrhage, a blood clot, or a tumor. We'll have to observe it over a period of time to see what it is."

It turned out to be a tumor, which grew in diameter as the weekly checkups went by. "But we don't know if it's a malignant tumor or not," the specialist said. "We'll need to do a biopsy."

Ten weeks had passed, and a lot of prayers had gone up for Dick's eye. Some people who came in to pray had asked God to totally heal his eye. I prayed that along with them. I didn't want him to lose the sight in his eye. I even prayed, "Lord, I want You to heal Dick's eye. I don't want him to lose it. Show me how much You care for me by making his eye well."

On November 22, I flew up to Houston and walked into the hospital, just as Dick was sailing by on the gurney en route to the operating room. I dashed after it to give him a quick kiss. The biopsy had showed cancer, so immediate removal of the eye was imperative. I was stunned. That was not the way I had prayed. Dick's brother Buddy and his wife Rosie were there. Rosie with her customary banter and upbeat attitude made me feel like I'd come to a birthday party during the hours we waited while he was in surgery.

It grew late, and Buddy and Rosie were ready to take me to accommodations for the night. I asked the nurse when could I see him. "Not until he's out of recovery," she said firmly.

"But I *need* to see him," I pleaded with her. "I'm his wife, and I just flew in from Mexico City. I came all this way just to be with him." She reconsidered, then led me down a hallway and into the dimly lit room. I stood gazing at him, lying there so still with a huge bandage over the place where his right eye had been. I said a prayer and gave him a gentle kiss on his forehead.

All the cancer was removed, being contained there in the eye. His recuperation went well, and he was fitted with an artificial eye. We spent a few days with my cousin Ray Wilkins and his family in Houston before returning to Mexico City. A month later we found ourselves at the annual OM Christmas campaign, held that year in Chihuahua.

The weather was cold and bleak that Christmas campaign in Chihuahua in 1974. It matched my mood. I was angry at God for not healing Dick's eye the way I asked Him to do. The boys, however, remember this as one of their happiest Christmases. We camped in our sleeping bags and electric blanket in one of the large unheated classrooms on the *Colegio Palmore* campus, where our entire team was housed. On Christmas Day it rained, sleeted, and snowed all in the same day. I taught the three boys how to fold paper in six sections and cut out their own snowflakes, the way my grandmother had taught me. We strung them up across the frigid classroom. We had already drawn a Christmas tree on the blackboard and stacked our gifts beneath it to open that morning.

Dick was doing well with his artificial eye. But I felt as though I were wandering in a gray fog spiritually. Did God really answer prayer? *Please, Lord, I prayed. Show me that you do answer prayer, and please bring me out of this grayness.* During the campaign I wrote down every prayer request anyone asked me to pray with them about, and I checked each off as the weeks went by and God answered prayers concerning everybody else.

Chihuahua Campaign. **Children in front :** *Philip, Steve, and Mark Griffin, Christa and Daniel Verwer. Dick and I are about fifth row back on the right.*

At campaign's end, we boarded a yellow school bus from Michigan loaded with college kids headed home—they had room for us. I called ahead to my mother that we were on the way, in case she would like to have breakfast ready. We made it into Booneville, Arkansas, for a hot southern breakfast of scrambled eggs, grits, sausage, and biscuits on New Year's morning, 1975. My mother had never served breakfast to a busload of hungry OMers before! Our boys talk about that campaign with that trip as their best ever.

At the end of February I went to a weekend women's conference in Mexico City, where Muriel Cook, a missionary for twelve years in Taiwan, was speaking. The first message about denying self left me humbled before God. The next one on prayer had words handcrafted from God for me. "When you pray, don't tell God how to answer," she said. "Place everything before Him in prayer, and then leave it with Him to answer in His own way." I spent that weekend weeping tears of repentance as the Lord showed me where I had been wrong. Not only had I told Him how to answer, but I also had demanded He prove His care for me by doing it my way. How could I ask Him to prove He cared for me when He had already demonstrated it beyond question in so many ways, the greatest of all in laying down His life for me. Moreover, He *had* healed Dick, not the way I demanded, but in His way, by seeing that all the cancer was removed. After that, I prayed for God to restore to me the fellowship I had known with Him before, so that I could walk always in intimacy with Him. In my spirit I felt Him say, *"I'm sending someone to help you."*

Later that year, 1975, we had a letter from an American couple, Jerry and Vicky Love, working with OM in Belgium. "God has put it on our hearts to come to Mexico for a year to help you in whatever way you may need us," they wrote. They arrived on

October 13, with true servants' hearts and set to work doing any and every task that needed to be done. Vicky was a real friend who knew how to listen and encourage. Extremely gifted, she taught piano to the boys, reupholstered the furniture, and along with Jerry did redecorating projects on the house and took care of all the meals. She substitute-taught for me whenever I needed her to at school or church and helped in myriad tasks with competence and a humble spirit. Moreover, being an author, she wrote a book later published by Bethany House titled *Childless Is Not Less*, about her own struggles with infertility.

At the Christmas campaign on the Nuevo Laredo/Laredo border, Jerry and Vicky were with us at the headquarters church on the Mexican side. Vicky was a servant to all. Besides her other duties, she commissioned herself to do the toilets, scrubbing them all twice a day so none of the team would pick up germs from dirty bathrooms. Vicky and I stayed up till 2:00 Christmas morning, chopping potatoes for a potato salad to feed the combined team of three hundred young people—150 on our side and 150 on the U. S. side—who would meet together for a day of prayer Christmas Day.

Once I had asked her to tell me their story. She had hesitated, knowing the policy in OM not to discuss issues that could be divisive. "Someday when it is the right time, I will," she said. That night as we diced potatoes I asked her again, and she did. As I listened, something deep inside me was stirred. Answers were there I'd been seeking, in regard to the Holy Spirit, although not in the form of words or logic, but of a

Person, and He was asking me for my response to Him. Deep in my spirit that post-midnight hour, I answered Him with one glad word: *Yes!*

As I walked under the still night sky across the courtyard back to the room where Dick and I were staying, my heart seemed to expand with joy. What is this? It was as though my heart had enlarged and was filling up with joy inside me. I remembered a verse in Psalm 119: "I will run the way of Thy commandments, when Thou shalt enlarge my heart." Dick and I had memorized that whole chapter together the year we were dating. I crawled in beside my sleeping husband that wee hour of Christmas morning with the wonder of it.

Over the following months the joy condensed into a flame of hope that burned inside me, a promise of what was coming, an expectation, an assurance. I spent time seeking the Lord, searching the Scriptures, repenting, and rectifying any relationship that wasn't right. Seeking to know the scriptural teaching on the subject of this experience with the Holy Spirit, I asked the Lord for guidance. John the Baptist baptized with water but proclaimed Jesus as the One who would baptize with the Holy Spirit and with fire. When Jesus came to John to be baptized, John objected saying, *"You come to me? I have need to be baptized of Thee."* He who was filled with the Holy Spirit from his mother Elizabeth's womb confessed to a need to be baptized of Jesus, the One who would baptize with the Holy Spirit and with fire. That became my prayer: *I have need to be baptized of Thee.*

Actually the terminology was not the important thing: it was the Person of the Lord Jesus Christ I was responding to, and His plan for me. Since it was taught in the churches where we were members throughout my childhood, it had left an indelible impression. I saw it primarily as the gift of a prayer language with which to worship God better, to intercede for others, and to know more of Him and His love.

Jerry and Vicky looked after the three boys when Dick and I flew to Europe for a month in the spring of 1976. Vicky also taught my class at Greengates and my Bible studies while we were away. The New Jersey office provided us with a special, two-week "Eu-Rail Pass" for boarding any train, anytime, going almost anywhere in continental Europe. It was a great adventure. Service was first-class, so we could have our private compartment and even lower our seats into a bed and sleep overnight. We visited OM teams in each country, enjoying the fellowship and getting to know the work there. We saw the breathtaking Alps in Austria and Switzerland, tulips beginning to blossom in Holland, and Dick's old army barracks in Frankfort, Germany. He was delighted they looked the same as when he lived in them from 1955 to 1957.

Then for the next two weeks we were on the MV/LOGOS, OM's first oceangoing ship. We sailed the Mediterranean from Italy to Spain during part of that time. Those days in our little berth on the ship gave me opportunity to talk to Dick. I had not yet told him my whole story of what God was doing in my heart, the roots of which traced back to the day I received Jesus when I was nine years old.

We had many hours to talk, pray, and open our hearts to each other. Dick was not in agreement at first but ended up accepting that this was God's will for me, though not necessarily for him. He thought the books written about it were shallow, and he did not sense a lack or a need in his own life as I did. As we left Spain heading back to Mexico, he was excited for me, anticipating what God would do.

Happy boys welcomed us at the Mexico City airport on our return home. Jerry and Vicky, who had been working with the Covenant Church along with OM that year, linked up with the Covenant Church to eventually serve full-time as their missionaries in Mexico.

Steve had got a brand-new yellow bicycle at Christmas while we were at the border. The Loves took it back to Mexico City for him on top of their van.

One afternoon he and his friends on the block were all out riding their bikes when it came a sudden downpour. The rain drenched him as he dashed back through the gate, hopped off his bike, and ran inside for shelter. I was in the living room with the ladies who'd gathered for Bible study. The pounding rain continued for a period during which all other sights and sounds from outside were diminished. When Steve went back out to get on his bike, it was gone.

Hurrying down the street, he discovered every bike on the block had been stolen. We later learned that a pickup truck had gone along gleaning a harvest of bicycles left in the yards by their young riders. The crafty thieves had taken advantage of the easy access to the bikes, along with the torrent of rain, to camouflage their movements.

Little Lost Dog

Philip loved June Bug, his little roly-poly puppy, the only offspring of his Pekingese, Frisky, and Steve's wiry, temperamental Chihuahua, Beetle Bug. I was there the morning June Bug was born. It was June 25. I was determined to assist in the birth, in the hope this one would survive. Frisky in her advanced age had given birth to her first puppy a year before, sired also by Beetle. That day we had been away, though, and returned to find Frisky with her lifeless puppy. We had to take it away, and she cried and searched for it many days. So the whole household rejoiced when June Bug was born. She had the Chihuahua body build and fair hair, and her Pekingese mother's flat black button nose and curly tail. She had one unusual feature, which I thought of as a birthmark: instead of an even number of teats on her tummy, she had seven.

Beetle was just four months old when we got him for Steve's eleventh birthday. Beetle was napping on my lap one evening shortly before I had to leave for an important PTA meeting at school to meet with the parents of the new children in my classroom. I playfully clucked my tongue at Beetle. He sprang into the air and bit the bottom of my nose! There was no way to bandage the wound. How embarrassed I was that evening conversing across the table with each set of dignified parents. June Bug, curiously, always showed her affection for me by a quick lick across the bottom of my nose as though to heal the very place bitten by her father when *he* was four months old.

When June Bug was four months old, she discovered she could flatten her little round body against the ground and squeeze under the front gate. One clear fall day she did this once too often. Philip and I searched the whole street for her in vain. We inquired of the neighbors next door on either side and across the street. No one had seen her. We asked people passing by. No, no one had seen our puppy. Philip was heartbroken. When the day was ending, he came to me and said, "Mommy, can we pray for God to bring June Bug back?"

Can we, Lord? I shot up a quick prayer in my heart to God. "Can I pray this with my son for You to bring his puppy home?" Strangely enough, I felt an inner peace, like a permission to go ahead. So Philip and I bowed our heads together and asked God to please bring June Bug back to us.

Days went by, then weeks and months. When June 25 rolled around the following year, I thought about June Bug with a little ache. I had pictures of her taken shortly before she disappeared. In one she posed princess-like. In another she lay curled in a tiny round ball on a pillow. I thought about pulling them out for the family and mentioning her birthday. But, no, that would be too painful for Philip. Besides, what about the prayer we had prayed together? So I didn't say anything.

Many more weeks went by. One Saturday morning Dick had taken the three boys out for their regular weekly fun time together. I was in the house alone with Frisky and Beetle when I heard someone knocking on the gate. A young boy was there. "Do you have any old newspapers to sell?" he asked. I started to tell him I had no newspapers but that I had some old telephone directories—when suddenly a little dog appeared and started scratching excitedly on the gate.

"Is that your dog?" the boy asked.

I only stared and thought, *What a cute little Chihuahua. My, but it really wants to come in!* Then out loud I said, "Would you like to buy the directories?"

The boy said he would. By that time Frisky and Beetle were going wild at the gate, and the little dog was yapping with abandoned glee. "I'll just let it in," I thought, puzzled. "It wants in so bad, and Frisky and Beetle are wanting it in, too."

I quickly lifted the latch and let it in and turned to go for the directories. The three dogs tore across the yard and flew through the house and out the back door. I collected the old telephone books and started to bend over to pick them all up when the strange little dog bounded back through the house with the other two, jumped straight at its target and licked me across the bottom of my nose.

"June Bug!" I yelled. I grabbed her out of the scramble, looked at her little white tummy and counted to seven. "Yes, it's June Bug!" I grabbed up the directories and ran to the gate. "Yes, it is my dog," I belatedly answered the boy. "Yes, it's my dog that has come home! Here, you can keep the directories,"

I said, thrusting them at him and dashing back into the house to hug June Bug.

What a rejoicing when the guys got home! Philip played all afternoon with his little dog. The next morning the three dogs were wrestling happily on the grass in the front yard when a neighbor from down the street knocked on the gate. "That's my dog," she said, pointing to June Bug. "Her name is Daisy."

"Oh, no. That's our dog," we replied. "Her name is June Bug."

We were both right. As we compared stories, we discovered that one day almost a year before some gardeners had knocked on her door offering to sell her the puppy. "It's a full-blood Chihuahua," they said. "See, you can tell by its curly tail."

She decided to buy the puppy for her young granddaughter's birthday and paid the men forty dollars. Her granddaughter lived in the south of Mexico City, and we lived in the extreme north. Almost a year had gone by. Then the granddaughter went on vacation to El Paso, and asked our neighbor to keep "Daisy" for her while she was away. The little dog escaped and came scratching on our gate.

After she heard our side of the story, saw how the three dogs were a close-knit little family, and observed how Philip was deeply attached to them, she said, "It's true. The dog is yours. I'm going to let you keep her. I only ask that when she has her first batch of puppies, you give us the pick of the litter." That's what we did.

One day I said to Philip, "Remember when you and I prayed and asked God to bring June Bug back?"

"Yes," he replied with a smile.

"Well, what did you think when so much time passed and she still had not returned?"

"I knew God would do it," Philip said.

* * *

In 1976 my dad repurchased the property in Grayson, Arkansas, he had owned in 1945 when we returned from California. Joyland Park it was called, but now it was joyless. The house with its country store had been rebuilt, but my dad hadn't been made over. His drinking, his raving, his insanity made everyone miserable. That summer he tore into me with objections to how Dick and I had raised Philip. Philip was a normal, active nine-year-old, full of life and fun. He loved people and thrived on challenging activities, so I was bewildered. What did my dad not like about him? Were active children too much for him to handle? Were those years of his own youth so painful that he could not bear seeing someone that age being joyful?

Searching my own heart, I wept. What had I done wrong? I had done everything I knew to do right and had prayed earnestly and continually for my three sons for God's wisdom in their upbringing. But my father's ranting unsettled me, and in my pain I said to Philip, "What have I done wrong in raising you?" Philip was extremely wounded by my words and what came down to him through me from his grandfather. In a move of reconciliation, he got a piece of wood and began whittling a present for me. In his eagerness, the knife slipped, and when he came to offer me his gift I ignored it, focusing only on his bleeding hand. I did not know it then, but the pain of my perceived rejection of both him and his gift cut deep into my son's spirit.

I observed the pain there over a long term, and the hurt in his eyes. I would ponder and wonder about what had caused it. But I did not know I was the one responsible for letting it pass down to him through me from generation to generation. Not until decades later did I learn and we were able to deal with the damage and repair the breach.

Another painful incident happened in Bulevares. While my ladies' weekly Bible study met in the living room, Philip was out riding his bicycle, but suddenly he appeared at the front door. I jumped up to see about him. There he stood, covered with mud and filth. I looked at him, and he gazed back at me, not saying a word. Then I said, "Philip, you're really dirty, you know? Why don't you go on back to the bathroom and get washed up." I felt his reluctance as he turned and went. If only I had gone after him and seen to him that very moment.

Not until many years later when Philip was studying for the ministry did I learn the complete story of what had transpired that afternoon and the devastating impact and long-term affects it had on him. The older boys who had attacked him, knocked him to the ground, kicked his bicycle to damage it, and called him derogatory names had also done a very humiliating thing: they had urinated on him.

I, who had always insisted with the women I taught that family comes first before ministry, had failed my own child that day by not taking time out, excusing myself, and looking after my son, who had been attacked physically and deeply hurt emotionally.

In the fall our landlord needed the Bulevares house for some of his family, and God provided a two-story house in the residential neighborhood of Pirules, a few miles to the north. Boxes were still stacked unpacked everywhere when Steve Hart arrived from OM's central accounting office in Belgium to audit the bookkeeping, which he did every five years.

Philip made friends right away with neighborhood boys, David and Miguel, up on the next corner. One day he dashed into the dining room where I was working, holding out a pencil and sheet of paper. "Mommy, quick! David wants to invite Jesus into his heart, and I don't know the words to pray with him. Please write down the words for me!" I did, and he hurried back up the street to their house. David gave his life to Jesus that day, and he is a pastor now, too, just like Philip.

Returning from the Christmas campaign in Monterrey in 1976, we were invited by David and Miguel's parents to cut the *Rosca de Reyes* bread with them for Three King's Day, the sixth of January. To my surprise I got the little plastic baby hidden inside, which meant I would invite everybody present for tamales on the second of February.

I don't think getting the baby in my portion of the *Rosca* meant I would get pregnant that night, *but I did.* So began a year mixed with more than sufficient grace for every trial. I had been on the birth control pill for almost nine years, but as soon as the doctor took me off of it because of swollen ankles, oops! You guessed it.

Mark's dream for many years had been to play American football and win a scholarship to pay his way through university. After all, his dad had earned a track scholarship to Mississippi State and even had an offer of a football scholarship from another school. So Dick told him that when he started tenth grade would be the time to go away to high school in the States.

The time came, but there was a problem. Mark and Steve had always done everything together and Steve could not bear the thought of Mark going away to school without him. So we were in the process of enrolling them both in French Camp Academy, a Christian school with boarding facilities in Mississippi.

During spring break from Greengates, we drove up as a family to visit the academy and then visit my parents in Arkansas, where we took Mark and Steve for their physicals. Dr. William Daniel at the clinic in Booneville called me into his office to say that our son Steve had a problem. My heart lurched. "What kind of problem?" I asked.

"His blood pressure is very high to his head and very low to his feet," he said. "He needs to see a heart specialist when you return to Mexico. I understand they have some of the best in the world."

"What do you think the problem is, Dr. Daniel?" I asked.

"I really couldn't say, since I'm not a specialist," he said.

"What do you *think* it might be?" I persisted. He told me what it could possibly be, and it turned out to be exactly what he described, an obstruction in the aorta artery.

Steve had surgery on April 26 in the Spanish Hospital in Mexico City. People around the OM world were praying for him. His cousin Dr. Thomas Griffin in Arizona called on the phone to counsel and prepare him for what to expect. The doctors said age thirteen was the ideal age to have this kind of surgery. Steve was a real soldier, and the operation was a total success.

We gave thanks to God for His hand in this. If we had not needed to get Steve's checkup, when would the problem have been discovered? If Steve had not insisted that he *must* go away to high school in the States when his bother Mark did, we would have taken only Mark for a physical exam.

I lost the baby seven days later at the ABC Hospital. Perhaps it was the trip and changes of altitude that had caused the umbilical cord to twist to a fine thread with the baby's turning. I asked Dr. Katz to let me see him. I was amazed at his little fingernails and everything so intricately formed at only four months. *My poor little son*, I acknowledged mentally, but I felt only numbness that morning.

It was not until a week later on Mother's Day that the emotion caught up with the reality. My little son had died. Grief swept over me, and I began to weep. Dick didn't quite know how to handle my sorrow and told me to stop crying, so I did, but all the tears for this child were dammed up inside me that night.

The next morning Regina, a girl on our team, pulled her Toyota into the driveway. She happened to be traveling from the south of Mexico up to the border, and God brought her on that very day. She sat on the edge of my bed, took my hand, and said, "Now you just cry all you need to." And I did, and healing began. Steve recovered swiftly and completely and within three weeks was back on the practice field with his football team.

Dick, Philip, and I were on our way over to French Camp that fall to check on Mark and Steve before returning to Mexico. We had left them there ten days before to begin their first year in boarding school. About lunch time Philip started campaigning for a hamburger. Dick reluctantly conceded that he would pull off at the next exit about fifteen miles up the road, Palestine, Arkansas. He needed to check the spare anyhow to be sure it had air. We were about to repent of having pulled off, when we saw the town was so tiny with little to offer. That's when Dick realized the right front tire was going flat, and we had just enough time to pull into the town's lone filling station to get it and the spare fixed. Moreover, a tiny hamburger stand offered delicious hamburgers. We would have been stranded on Interstate 40 if Philip had not insisted! That was our only flat on the whole trip.

The first person to greet us when we arrived on the French Camp campus about suppertime was the school nurse. Steve had awakened that morning with a fever and was at the doctor's about twenty-seven miles away. We drove on toward Mark's dorm. "Boy, am I glad you're here!" was his joyous greeting as he came bounding out, exploding with exciting news: first-string running back, sports editor for the *Panther Print* (school newspaper), letter from a new friend he had met in Stuttgart, three hours daily in the kitchen, washing dishes and emptying smelly garbage, roommate Rob accepted Christ, jogging five miles at 5:30 every morning, military-strict rules and discipline. "Just *ask* me anything! What *hasn't* happened? Just ask me *anything!* Oh, yes," he said, "singing bass in the chorus and probably going on tour." The only sad note was that he hardly got to see Steve, and Steve wasn't happy and didn't want to stay.

Pale, teary-eyed Steve appeared, accompanied by Carlos Haro who had played little league football with them in Mexico, and we all walked over to the dining hall. Steve had no appetite but drank his iced tea and ate all his fruit plus mine. After supper we got the dean of students' permission to take the boys to Greenville for the weekend. Steve slept most of the three-hour trip, while Carlos sat meditatively, Philip asked questions, Mark talked, and Dick and I listened. It was nice to be together. We piled in on Davis and Helen and their little grandson for the night, pretty exhausted.

The next afternoon, we all went bowling. (I won't tell my score, but everybody beat me!) Dick asked if I would get alone with Steve and try to get to the bottom of his problem. He had tried a couple of times, but Steve had only ended up in tears. So Steve angled across the bed in a spare bedroom in Dick's mother's house, and I sat on a footstool and listened. It was the rules, the kids, the classes, the coach, the boss at his work assignment. Nothing was as he expected, and he hardly ever got to see Mark. He had tried to tell his dad all that was wrong, and his dad said to stick in there and not give up and later he would be glad. "Why?" he said. "That would be like, keep on banging your head against a wall and you'll be glad when you stop."

The six of us drove to a lookout on the Mississippi River, and I reported to Dick everything Steve had said. Then he, Mark, Steve, and I all conferred together around a picnic table, and prayed for wisdom for the right decision, each one of us offering a prayer.

It was an extremely difficult decision for us to make, and we didn't make it until the last minute—Tuesday evening before we left on Wednesday morning. We wanted to do the correct thing and the best thing for Steve. Would it be right to take him out? Would we be helping him develop a pattern of irresponsibility if we let him drop out because it didn't suit his fancy? This especially concerned us because Dick had let him quit football in the summer and go with him on the campaign. The coach had been working Steve harder than the other guys to get him caught up because he had entered late on account of his operation, and Steve just wasn't able to take it, neither did we think it best for him.

We knew Tuesday evening, though, during a special family supper together in Mark's dorm (pizzas and peaches!) that we had made the right decision to take Steve back to Mexico with us. The staff and teachers were in agreement. His classmates were the reluctant ones. They had elected him dorm representative before we got there and on Monday had chosen him as their class reporter for the newspaper and they did not want him to leave.

I have seen how this worked out for the best in so many ways. (1) I was half as sad as I would have been, with one son away instead of two! (2) Steve had to learn sometime that God had different things in store for him than He had for Mark. They had always done everything together until this year, and a lot of things I know Steve did because they were Mark's interests and he wanted to be with Mark, not because they were particularly his interests. (3) It was so good for Philip to have Steve. Philip had always been the overachiever, determined to keep up with the other two, even though he's five years younger than Mark and three and a half years younger than Steve. He and Steve became real companions and found themselves compatible; moreover, Steve learned leadership qualities, being the older sibling. (4) Steve reentered Greengates and his various activities with a new, appreciative attitude and definitely profited from the whole experience.

Our trip back was wet. We stopped the first night in a little town called Winnie, east of Houston. The three small towns south of Winnie were evacuating to the north because of Hurricane Anita, so I think we got the last vacant motel room, even though it was still early. Once we crossed the border into Mexico, we had constant rain except for a letup of thirty minutes or less, so driving was slow and I didn't enjoy the blurry view through the windshield when the wiper on my side stopped functioning! The luggage on top was covered with a yellow canvas, but it couldn't be held responsible for keeping everything dry, and some items became damp and slightly unglued, one of them being Dick's Bible.

More wetness awaited us on arriving home, because the back room, which served for laundry and storage, had been flooded with several inches of water. When I finished sorting through everything, I was sorry to have to discard many black and white photos from my high school days.

I didn't miss teaching school, although I thought I would. With the opportunity to take more Bible study groups for women across the city, my week was filled with what I truly loved doing. I remember when I started teaching at Greengates, I thought to myself, *This is the nicest thing that could happen to me!* Then seven years later when I stopped teaching, I realized I felt the same way: *This is the nicest thing that could happen to me!*

In October of that year I had one particular week of intensive intercession for my dad. "Oh, Lord," I prayed, "if only he could be well. If only he could be whole." I remembered stories he had told of his childhood—the way his mother held him close to her just before she died. He was only six years old when he followed the wagon with the roughly hewn coffin to Lick Creek Cemetery. I thought of the double abandonment he felt the next morning on discovering his grandmother had gone back to Arizona when she'd said she would take him with her, his father's cruelty, and the hunger and poverty in rural Arkansas during the Great Depression with nothing to eat but field corn fried, but without any oil, by his stepmother Mary.

"Dear Lord, if only my dad could be whole." The sufferings had dug deep into who he was. Near the end of that week, I was interceding with intense longing for him to be well. I prayed, "Lord, I know it isn't possible, but if only I could have been in his place. If only I could have suffered all that instead of him so that he could be whole!"

I knew my longing was sincere, my desire real, but at the same time impossible, maybe even ridiculous; nevertheless I prayed it. "If only I, instead of him, so he could be well!"

Then I felt the Lord say to me, *"You don't have to. I already did."* Lines from Isaiah's prophecy of Christ's suffering came to my mind.

Surely our griefs He Himself bore,
And our sorrows He carried...
The chastening for our well-being fell upon Him,
And by His scourging we are healed.
(Isaiah 53:4a, 5b, NASB)

What I was intensely longing for, Jesus had already done. He had suffered it already. My dad could now be whole, because Jesus had taken his place and borne his griefs and sorrows. Taking that word, I prayed, "Lord, You bore his hurt already. I place his grief and sorrow there on You on the cross, where you already suffered it two thousand years ago—and my dad goes free!

Later I learned that Mother had also been praying diligently and having others pray for him during that very same period. He had stopped drinking for several weeks, and her hopes were very high. Then suddenly one night, November 19, her hopes came crashing down when he was helped home in a drunken stupor. Her church was having a special series of meetings that week. She decided to go but sat on the very back row in her despondency. At the end of the message, the visiting preacher said, "If there is someone here tonight with a heavy heart, please come forward so we can pray for you."

My mother thought, There is no one here with a heavier heart than mine. I'm going!

The minister had her sit in a chair as proxy for my dad and prayed for him. God heard that prayer, along with mine and many others, and that was a major turning period for him.

God is able to make him stand.

Christmas 1977, Saltillo. Steve, Mark, Philip in front; Dick and Helen behind them.

Over four hundred of us converged on Saltillo that Christmas of 1977: roughly 150 Canadians, 140 Americans, and 130 Mexicans. Saltillo was celebrating a quadricentennial. It was four hundred years since Spain conquered Mexico and founded this city in the mountains about fifty miles southwest of Monterrey. OM had opened its first bookstore there in 1958 on the very first Christmas campaign. The first 18 eager students from Moody, Wheaton, and Emmaus had arrived then, contrasted with 418 this Christmas.

Mark was back from his first semester at French Camp Academy, and we were all together as a family again. You can see how contented I look in the picture!

We gave the boys a small allowance to buy gifts for each other. They pooled their pesos to buy a gift for their dad and a gift for me. We still treasure his leather tripod stool and my wooden *relievo* of a Mexican kitchen.

We got back from the Christmas campaign in Saltillo, and on a Thursday morning in early January, I called my assistant leader of the Spanish Bible study I led in the Satelite area.

"I need this morning alone to pray," I told Linda Buenfil, and she was glad to fill in. I went up to my room and knelt by the window. It had been two years since the flame was lit in my heart, and I had waited on God for His answer. That morning I began to pray in a new language I had asked Him for two years before on Christmas Eve. I had several reasons for asking for it, but whittled my list down to three, then to only two: for worshiping Him better and for interceding in prayer for others.

As I worshiped that morning, my mind and spirit seemed to expand to comprehend more of the wonder of who God is, greater and wider than the expanding heavens. Then as I interceded for my dad, it were as though I saw inside his brain, disorderly, chaotic, scattered, like the broken contents of a child's toy box flung across the floor. As I prayed I watched the fragmented parts move into their proper places, fitting together piece by piece to make one whole—a healing in his mind.

There they were: the worship and the intercession. The third reason, which I had eventually put aside, not wanting to risk asking selfishly, was to know personally more of the greatness of His love for me. *I was to begin to find out something about that one later.*

Across India

Dick and I left for India on January 19, 1978, invited by OM the year before to visit the teams across the subcontinent. At first Dick was reluctant because many people we knew who had gone there were sick every day, but I was thrilled at the idea of the trip and encouraged him. When we arrived in Bombay, however, the shock of leprosy, poverty, filth, whole families living and sleeping on the sidewalks, overwhelming multitudes of people glutting the cities, and the palpable spiritual shackles of Hinduism made me vacillate. *I can't travel across India, I thought. I won't make it. I'll die halfway.*

The next day we walked up the gangplank of the LOGOS, which was in Bombay for dry dock. We were seated at a table out on the deck with the Indian leader. He laid our itinerary in front of us, and I ran my eyes down the schedule. *Everything is for Dick,* I thought. There's nothing here for me. I'll just be his shadow and never open my mouth. It was a fiery dart from the enemy to add to my misgivings, but I allowed it entry.

Dick's first assignment was to preach that weekend in the state of Gujarat. He went with a translator from the ship to buy our train tickets and came back to say tickets were all sold out. "But people without tickets force themselves onto the train any way they can," the translator said, "therefore it might be best that just Brother Dick and I go, if you don't mind staying on the ship for the weekend?" I was delighted. The ship was a haven of cleanliness, and I had already thought in my culture-shocked state how wonderful it would be to stay on it and sail around India up to Calcutta, instead of journeying overland.

I was assigned to the vacant second lieutenant's cabin on the deck, and no one bothered me that whole weekend. People just brought a bite of food when they thought I might want it, leaving me to rest and recover from the eleven-and-a-half-hour time change between Mexico and India. God shut me up in that cabin away from the thoroughfare that weekend because He had some work to do on me. First of all, He had me turn loose of everything, piece by piece, one by one, as though it would never be mine again.

1) My own life. So what, if I got sick and died halfway across India? If that was His plan for me, so be it.
2) My husband, away on a weekend preaching trip. Release him.
3) My three sons, all being cared for by others while we were on this six-week trip. Surrender Mark, a student in French Camp, Mississippi, and Steve living with Bob and Jean Clement in Valle Dorado, and Philip with Tom and Elizabeth Bennett in Mexico City. Give each of them over to God. They were not mine to hold on to.

4) My six Bible studies for women throughout Mexico City, all in the care of other teachers while I was gone. Turn them loose forever. Let the other women take them permanently.
5) My responsibilities as a missionary with OM. Give everything back to Him: everything else I did in leading, serving, and training others.
6) My disappointment on seeing the itinerary. So what, if I were only Dick's shadow? That was all right. I would be there beside him, supporting him, praying for him. That would be me, a shadow.

God dealt with me deeply on each issue. There in the stillness after I'd surrendered the totality of all I was, and had, and did, over to Him, I felt stripped of everything and empty-handed too. I didn't like the feeling. That's when He spoke into my spirit, *"I wanted you to come to this place, because I have something to say to you."*

"Something to say to me?"

"Yes. I want you to know that I love you, the essential you, apart from who you are in relationship to other people: wife, mother, teacher, missionary. Apart from anything you do for Me, I love YOU." I was absolutely amazed at the words. I have never been so deeply touched by LOVE.

The next morning I came out of my cabin for the first time, for Sunday worship. The small, multinational group of OMers left on board, seated around dining tables on the deck with the waters of the

Arabian Sea splashing against the vessel, blended their accents to sing:

*Redeemed to worship Him, redeemed to praise His name,
Out of every tribe and nation,
Redeemed to worship Him, redeemed to praise His name,
Out of every kindred and tongue.*

Dave Hicks, ship director, led the meeting. At one point he said, "If God has done something special in your life in these last few days, please share it with the group." He seemed to be gazing right at me. *Oh, no*, I thought. *This is way too personal.* He kept on looking my way. "If God has done something, then don't deprive the rest of us. Tell us." So I did, but not without choking up when I got to the part about His love, I was so deeply stirred.

Later I silently prayed, *"Lord, You don't have to, but if you could, please confirm to me that I really did the right thing in sharing that."*

We disbanded and were preparing to leave the ship when a girl from Germany came up to me. "I want to thank you!" she said. "You'll never know how much God ministered to me through what you shared about His love. Thank you." *Thank You, Lord.*

Dick returned from the weekend preaching trip in Gujarat. Monday morning we said goodbye to the OM team at the base in Bombay. I snapped a picture of them with the Loves' camera loaned to me to take slides. The tickets in our hands didn't keep us from having to force our way onto the train. People. Unimaginable crowds of humanity everywhere. A sea of people every direction I turned. Even Mexico City with its millions and its crowded subway system didn't compare. We pushed our way onto a train going to Indore. I was a little nervous on the way. Was I ready for this? But that ride was the beginning of the most amazing trip of my life.

Nobody stirred at the compound in Indore, where I was abandoned in the middle of India to wait for Brenda Taylor, leader of the girls' team, to pick me up. Dick had left for eleven days on a preaching tour with Victor, his translator. The men's team leader, Madhu Das, who'd just served us a delicious rice and vegetable dish he'd prepared, was nowhere to be seen.

Alone again, I stood there in the middle of the large compound. Then I heard soft singing coming from the church. I crept in and found a seat toward the back. It was beautiful. My second worship experience in India had a feel of eternity in it, as though one could worship God forever without a time limit. Was that because I was free of any obligation or preoccupation? I knew it was more than that. I could tell the group in there also felt it.

They were a team called Christ is the Answer, and it was a day of prayer and fasting. They prayed, they sang, and they also confessed offenses to one another and asked for forgiveness. When they did that, I thought, *Oh, no! They won't like it that I'm in here, hearing these personal confessions regarding relationships on their team. When they notice I've come in, they're going to ask me to leave.*

But they didn't. In fact, they were glad to see me and asked me to introduce myself. "I'm with Operation Mobilization," I said. "My husband and I just arrived from Mexico to visit the OM teams across India." They were delighted and started streaming toward me with hugs and warm greetings. Jamon, their leader, was from Arkansas! Edna, with her two sons, was from Litchfield, Illinois, where my dad had worked in the coal mines. Edna and I became friends immediately. The fellowship with that team and the friendship with Edna seemed to fill my heart with a joy unspeakable. It must have been the joy Jesus promised when we are loving one another. *"These things I have spoken to you, that My joy may be in you, and that your joy may be made full. This is My commandment, that you love one another just as I have loved you"* (John 15:11-12 NASB).

That first evening Brenda Taylor, behind the wheel of the OM team's van, maneuvered us through Indore traffic, spiced with water buffalo, cows, rickshaws, and city buses. She skillfully avoided people and smaller animals, as she turned her head briefly to look at me. "We're scared," she said.

"Why?" I asked.

"There's this man in the government who invited us to his home tonight to ask questions about Christianity. We're afraid we won't have answers," she looked at me imploringly. "Will you come with us?"

"Yes, I can go with you," I said. The gentleman had invited two friends from his office, plus his wife and two teenaged daughters. Brenda seated me facing him, while she and her assistant leader, Hema, took the background. From the very first question which started with creation and went through the Bible, I thought, Lord, I don't know how to answer this man. But two things happened I have never experienced apart from that night. The Holy Spirit opened my understanding of what he was really asking and gave me answers for him. And as I spoke, I felt an almost overwhelming love of God for this Baha'i man. Question after question after question, the whole room was attentive, listening, for three solid hours.

Back in the van, again behind the wheel, Brenda gave a great sigh. "Aren't you just exhausted after a session like that?" she asked.

It's true we had gone three hours, but I was surprised myself at the elation I was feeling, and I said to Brenda, "Wow, it's strange, but instead of depleted, I actually feel energized." It was then I realized the principle of working together with God. When I operate out of the Holy Spirit's power, the person receiving from Him through me is ministered to, and I also am built up.

The next morning Hema came into the sitting room where I was reading. "May I ask you a question?" she said. When I indicated yes, she continued. "Is God partial? Does He love some people more than others?"

"Why do you ask that, Hema?"

"Well, my father loves my brother more than me. He says my brother is smart and I am stupid. My mother loves my sister more than me. She says my sister is beautiful and I am ugly."

"No, God is not partial," I said. "He loves you as though you were the only one He had to love." I told her how our human love can be faulty and limited and conditional: "I will love you if you are good," or "I love you because you please me." "But God's love is not like our human love," I said. "His love for us is perfect, unconditional, unchanging, without measure, and without end. God says, 'I love you, Hema. You are the only one of you I have to love. And I love you perfectly.'"

Thinking on the conversation later, I realized I'm the only one of *me* who can love Him back. Love goes two ways. He has poured His love into my heart, with which also I am *to love Him*. If I don't do it, no one else can do it for me, and He misses out. This same love also automatically flows out to others.

I had pondered while still back in Mexico before making this trip what the women of India were like. What kinds of things were important to them? What did they think about? What kinds of questions did they have? During my eleven days with Brenda and her team, I discovered they are the same as we are, though perhaps with even more depth. They deal with many of the same questions, have the same kinds of emotions and longings, want to be taught and prepared for life, for marriage, for serving God. They even requested a series on sex education because many were facing marriages arranged by their parents without any preparation at all.

One afternoon I borrowed Brenda's typewriter and wrote a letter to each of my three sons. I thought of each one and how they are so different, and at the end of each letter I wrote a special note.

To my firstborn, the striver, the perfectionist, I wrote, "Mark, I love you apart from all your achievements and the excellence you pursue. You are of infinite value just as you are."

To my middle son, whose identity was so linked with that of his older brother, doing everything together, I wrote, "I love you, Steve, the unique individual God has made you to be."

To my youngest, alert and active and often getting into trouble, I wrote, "Philip, I love you. Sometimes you get yourself into scrapes, but my love for you does not change."

Brenda asked me if I was ready to speak to the nurses at the hospital. I was ready. I entered a conference room packed with light brown faces in a sea of white uniforms. Brenda brought me here to the hospital by invitation. They gazed at me expectantly as I walked up to the podium. "Jesus Christ is Lord of all" was the theme of my talk. He is Lord of the universe and Lord in my life. I told them how He is coming again to earth to reign as Lord and King.

"Every knee is going to bow and every tongue is going to confess that Jesus Christ is Lord," I said. Everyone listened wide-eyed and attentive. They didn't want a short devotional. They were hungry to hear more about this Jesus. So I continued talking about Him.

When I finally concluded, I said, "You have an opportunity now to make Him Lord, and surrender your life to Him. He *is* Lord, whether you choose to recognize Him as such or not. That is your choice. But one day *your* knee also is going to bow to Jesus Christ the LORD OF ALL."

Eyes did not move away from me, watching, ears listening. I imagined each one of them recognizing Jesus Christ as Lord and bowing in reverence. I can still see their faces, though I snapped no photograph. I still pray for that roomful of nurses.

A printed sheet of paper hung on the screen door of the missionary's house in Balasore, India. It was a prayer. I came up close to read.

> *Dear God,*
> *Make the door of this house wide enough*
> *To receive all who need human love,*
> *Fellowship and the Father's care,*
> *And narrow enough to shut out envy, pride and hate.*
> *Make its threshold smooth enough*
> *To be inviting to children and straying feet,*
> *But rugged enough*
> *To turn back the tempter's power.*
> *Dear God,*
> *Make the door of this house*
> *The gateway*
> *To Thine eternal kingdom.*

I copied it down and tucked it into my suitcase. *I like this. I want to put it on my door.*

This American missionary, Sue Powers, invited me to speak to her courtyard full of school children that first afternoon and again the following morning. She came into the house afterward carrying a special treat. "You must try some of India's sweets," she said. It was our only time to taste the delicious candy of India.

When we had a few minutes to talk, I asked her, "Sue, how does a missionary survive here? How does one handle the extreme conditions?"

"Some can't," she said. "They shut themselves inside their compound and don't go out."

Sadly enough, I could understand. There I was, two weeks earlier, wanting to stay on the ship and sail *around* India.

We traveled across India those six weeks, each carrying one small suitcase. It had not been a problem for me until one day on a train platform none of the doors were open for us to board. Dick did not take the situation standing still. He raced us back and forth, back and forth, back and forth, up and down that long terminal, determined to find an open door. I grew weary and irritable and began to complain that I needed to stop. But he could not listen, and he could not stop, and when we finally at last were able to board, I vented my frustration on him.

Standing there was a quiet gentleman, and we three entered our compartment to take our seats. Wow! How did we get into first class? As I climbed up into the bunk overhead, Dick began immediately to talk to the man about Jesus.

"I have never seen Him," the man said. I was struck to the core.

"Forgive me, Lord," I prayed. "He certainly has not seen You reflected in me."

In a rickshaw with Dick on a starry night down a country lane to the team house outside Balasore, the words of a Bill and Gloria Gaither song hummed through my mind:

*"We have these moments to hold in our hand,
And to touch as they slip through our fingers
like sand.
Yesterday's gone and tomorrow may never come,
But we have these moments today."*

It was a timeless moment, one of the most precious of my life, fully in touch with God's creation, and with India, and the wonder of being alive in a place where time touched eternity.

Something troubled me at the OM men's team house, though, and I couldn't put my finger on what it was. "Please pray for me," I said to Dick. "I'm supposed to speak to this group of women who are coming in, and I can't."

"The Spirit is willing, but the flesh is weak," Dick said in a gentle rebuke.

"Actually, in myself," I said. "I am wanting to and willing to do it. But something is blocking."

Dick prayed for me, and I went into the room where all the women had gathered. I'm glad they were all inside and safely seated, because immediately a fierce hailstorm came down such as I had never seen before. I looked out the window and wanted to weep. I watched in horror as people dashed for cover while the wind blew and golf-ball-sized hailstones pounded their frail frames.

I taught the women for one hour from the book of Romans about our great salvation and thanked God for giving me the freedom to do it. The next morning I saw what had been blocking me.

After breakfast Dick went out in evangelism with the men. Then I was told by the team leader and his wife to go upstairs to the left and see a girl who was separated from everyone in a room at the far end of the building.

"There's a girl here?" I said, surprised.

"Yes," they answered. "She was a girl's team leader. Something happened. They don't know what. She had to be sent away. She is in total isolation here."

I found Esther lying on a little cot. Paralyzed. "What happened to you?" I asked.

I spent that whole week with Esther, while Dick worked with the team of men. She and I prayed for the physical afflictions and paralysis, but most of all for the spiritual bondage.

"My grandmother," she said, "put a curse on my father. He went crazy and had to be tied to a tree. There he died." She didn't know if some of that curse had passed down to her.

The problem on the team started, she said, when they did a production of C. S. Lewis's *The Screwtape Letters*. She played the part of Screwtape, representing Satan. Somehow the anger and hatred she portrayed in the play took over in her. They had to send her away.

God gave us the time, that entire week, and the place, that little isolated room, to pray through everything in Esther's life. God healed her physically from the paralysis and other ailments she was being medicated for. He also set her free from the demonic influences on her. Instead of a pale, paralyzed girl lying on a cot in an empty, isolated room, she came out radiant and joyful, as from a tomb, grave clothes unwound.

"I want to go with you to the ship in Calcutta," she begged. "Please take me with you."

I contacted Cathy Hicks, wife of the ship's director. "No! I do not want her on the ship!" Cathy said. I then told her about the week and what had transpired.

"Her will must be totally submitted to God," Cathy said, "I do not want her to even set foot on the ship unless she has surrendered her will unconditionally to Him."

"That's good," I told her. I knew that was the key to her remaining free.

Dick and I took Esther with us when we left on the train to Calcutta. I turned her over to Cathy. She later entered Bible school. The last I heard from her she was translating the Scriptures into one of the multitudinous languages of India.

If God sent me to India just for Esther, it was worth it.

Esther Kishore, a team member, and Dick.

"I feel it's very important we have time with Abel," I had said to Dick at different times as we worked our way across India toward Calcutta. Abel Ventura was our only Mexican working abroad that year. We had seen him briefly in Bombay on the ship Logos. He showed us the tiny room where single-handedly he ran the ship's only printing press. "We need to update him on Mexico," I said. "and also get news from him to take back with us." Dick agreed.

When we climbed on board the ship, Dick went to the ship's leaders and got permission to take Abel on a scenic bus tour of Calcutta. We had a whole day together, riding the bus and getting off to see the city and the tourist sights. We talked. We prayed for

Mexico. We prayed for Abel's family back in Mexico and Abel's goals for the future.

Picnic in Chapultepec Park, Mexico City. Abel on far right in 1976 before he left to serve on the M/V Logos. Norma, Enrique, Carl, Eunice, Oli, Pablo, Danny, Philip, Steve, Helen, Mark, Abel.

I fell in love with India and wept for India when we returned to Mexico. OM had dubbed it, "The land where the need is surpassed only by the opportunity." The need, both spiritual and physical, was overwhelming. The culture shock I felt on returning to Mexico was even greater than on arriving in India. In comparison to India, Mexico was rich! Mexico had everything! India's need was desperate, dire, and to my mind it was incomprehensible that both could exist on the same planet, that both could be reality. That was true culture shock.

I wrote a short piece about India soon after my return, called "Sensational India."

Gentle, sweet, spicy, jarring, and unrecognizable aromas were my first impression on arriving in Bombay's international airport before dawn that February morning. My pen stumbled on the notepad in an effort to identify even one of the smells. "Tar ... blacktop perking in a caldron," I wrote. All the others were a bouquet as strange as the multitude of languages spoken around me. My nose was charmed and mystified.

We left the expansive airport behind and headed toward the city of ten million. In the distance the lights of Bombay shone in a pitch-black shroud of night. Plain lights, like little stars cracking the darkness, caused me to remark on the beauty. "Actually, this is the best time to see the city," replied Jeremy, our British chauffeur, "when all you can see are the lights." Later I understood his wry comment. Even before reaching the compound, the headlights of his car uncovered a shocking panorama—people sleeping along the streets and on the sidewalks. The message my eyes captured jolted my entire system.

Whenever Jeremy met another car, he honked. "Why are you honking?" I asked. I wanted to say, "Please don't honk! Can't you see the people are asleep? You're going to wake them up!" But I didn't, and the people didn't rouse.

"It's the custom here," Jeremy replied. "When you meet another car at night, you honk." My ears felt assaulted in the clear stillness.

Arriving at the guest center, we were shown to our room by an Indian couple, who immediately retired. It was 4:00 in the morning. We plopped down on the narrow couch bed, but I realized how thirsty I was after the long plane flight and got up in search of water. "Don't drink the water," Dick said.

"But I have to drink something. I'm terribly thirsty," I said. I poked around the kitchen area adjacent to our room. Hooray! There was a big ceramic water dispenser with a spout. In the dim light I reached for a mug, filled it with life-giving water, and went back to our quarters.

"Don't drink the water," Dick said again. I then looked into my cup and got my second shock of the day— a huge cockroach! My thirst didn't get scared away, but, thankfully, Dick discovered a tangerine—a tasty, juicy, luscious delight to my taste buds and partial quencher of my thirst.

Sleep was rich and satisfying, and on awakening we were served porridge, like a thick cream of wheat. No, I could not eat it with my bare hand the Indian way. My mind said that fingers did not go into food. Wait. Give me some time. Let me use a spoon for now. Several days went by, actually, before I got up the nerve at one dinner meal to plunge my fingers into the steaming curried vegetables over rice. It was like jumping off a high, overhanging cliff into deep water below. I didn't drown right there in front of everybody. In fact, the exquisiteness of touching the flavorful food and placing it between your lips with living utensils instead of a cold, uncaring fork had no comparison. A tingling new dimension had been added to touch and taste.

That first weekend in Bombay offered more sight and olfactory experiences than my brain was ready to receive. Even eighteen years in Latin America had not prepared me for the lepers, the filth, the stench of open sewage canals in people's front doors, the extreme poverty of the multiplied millions of beautiful, brown-skinned, sensitive souls created in God's image.

Some people had said there were four rats for every person in India, while some said six. Others said the rats ate enough to feed all of Canada. Someone chased a black one the size of a rabbit out of the kitchen. I watched, cringing. "Why do you not kill them?" I asked. Shrugs.

When I swatted a mosquito on my arm, one of the Indian girls said quietly, "Do they bother you?" I would donate blood, but I didn't want what the insects offer me in return; so I gulped down chlorine-laden drinking water with my tiny white malaria pills.

Back in Mexico, when Dick and I had first received the invitation to India, he was reluctant. But I encouraged him. "Oh, I want to go! Please, let's accept!" With my eagerness Dick eventually was won over. But now I was backing down. We were scheduled to travel by train across India from Bombay to Calcutta, making stops along the way. "We'll get halfway across India," my mind said to me, "and I will die. I will not make it."

Instead of dying, however, I became more alive in India than I had ever been in my life, and neither of us was sick a single day. All my senses were heightened to perceive and receive on an almost ethereal level during that six-week journey.

I touched moments in India ... and drank in country scenes ... and heard the radiant colors of the saris ... and tasted oriental melodies ... and beheld the glory of timelessness ... and wafted in the fragrance of a beautiful, hospitable nation of people. It was sensational!

* * *

Back in Mexico City in March, the telephone rang. It was Linda calling from Tulsa.

"Helen! Mama and Daddy's fortieth wedding anniversary is April 9, and we're planning for all five of us kids to be there for a surprise celebration. They don't know anything about it. Alton is coming, too—they haven't see him for five years! You've got to come! Please say that you can!

Dick had other commitments, but the three boys and I attended. The whole family gathered there in the Mt. Sinai Assembly of God Church in Sugar Grove, Arkansas, where they first gave their hearts to Jesus and began their spiritual journey when I was six months old. The prayer my mother and I had prayed twenty years before, kneeling beside her bed and agreeing together, God had begun to answer.

On that Sunday morning of their anniversary, my dad stood up in the little church and said, "All of you here know me. You know what kind of life I have lived, and I am not proud of it. I want you to know that I have turned my life back over to Jesus Christ to live for Him." His desire was sincere, and he did resume his spiritual journey with some good, albeit sporadic fits and starts.

40th Wedding Anniversary. Linda, Joyce, Alton, Helen, Jimmy, James, and Dorothy.

Back in Mexico, the telephone rang on July 26, 1978, as I sat at the big wooden desk by the front window of our house in Pirules. It was Dave Hicks calling from Taiwan. "Abel drowned," he said. "He was in swimming with his ship 'family,' and some of the guys got into dangerous waters. Locals standing on the shore yelled to warn them. The others were able to get out, but Abel's head struck a rock in the undertow as he was pulled under."

Dick called Abel's sister, Gilberta, who worked as a nurse at the *Hospital La Raza*, in the north end of Mexico City to notify her. Gilberta had been on campaigns with OM in Italy. The family wanted his body brought back for burial in their village down in the state of Oaxaca. Three weeks later when his body finally arrived back to his homeland, his sister Gilberta stood up in the funeral home in Mexico City and told of Abel's decision to go into missions. He had finished university and knew God's call was on his life. In Mexico the son who has a career is expected to work and help support his parents. So he said to his sister, "I love my parents and would gladly give my first ten years to them, but I don't know how long I have; therefore, I must give my first years to God."

Paul Troper from the New Jersey office flew down for the funeral in Abel's native village of Tetela, Oaxaca. That day at the memorial service, many people who were impacted by Abel's life believed on Christ as their Savior. A few days later a letter reached us that Abel had posted shortly before his death. In it he had written this verse: "I press toward the mark for the prize of the high calling of God in Christ Jesus." That winter when the "Second Ship" arrived in Mexico, the challenge was given: "Who will take Abel's place?" A total of fourteen Mexican young people boarded the ship M/V *Doulos* to replace Abel and take the gospel message around the world. *If a grain of wheat falls into the ground and dies, it bears much fruit.*

One week in the fall of 1978, in the aftermath of Abel's death, I was having an especially difficult time. Every day that week was heavy and oppressive.

Dick was out of town, and spiritual battles seemed fierce. At the end of the week, I prayed, "Lord, if only I knew someone was praying for me, it would really help."

Sometimes while going through a difficult time, I would get a phone call from Linda. She would say, "What's happening? I've been having a burden to pray for you." Or I would get a letter from someone saying he or she was praying and wanting to know how things were going. I watched for the postman. But no letter came. I waited for the telephone to ring. No call either.

That afternoon I was leaning over the kitchen sink washing dishes, when I clearly felt the Lord say to me, *"I'm praying for you."*

Wow! I lifted my head up. "Oh, thank You, Lord Jesus! What more could I ask than to know that *You* are praying for me!"

With that all the burdens of the week lifted, and my heart was free. "And what are you praying, Lord?" I dared to ask. His words to Peter flashed into my mind: *"That your faith fail not."*

A few weeks later a farewell luncheon was held for one of the ladies from church who was leaving Mexico. It was out in the country, so some of us parked our cars at the suburban Lomas Verdes shopping center and rode together in just a few cars.

After the luncheon one of the gals, Mary Alice, said, "Helen, would you ride back with me to get your car? There's something I want to tell you. On the drive back, holding the steering wheel with one hand, she reached into her pocket with the other and pulled out a piece of paper. "I don't know if these dates will mean anything to you," she said, handing me the note, "but I just wanted to tell you that *every* day that week I was praying for you." I looked at the paper. It was the exact same week! *YOU give abundantly above all we ask or think.*

Christmas of 1978 aboard the M/V *Doulos* was exciting because Mark arrived again for the campaign—and this time to the ship, docked in Tampico on the Gulf coast. Mark came bearing gifts from the name-drawing: Jimmy got mine, Mona got Dick's, Mike got Mark's, Joel got Steve's and Stephanie got Philip's. Mother had sent money to Mark, and he had used it to buy a physics' set for Philip and record albums for Steve, Dick, and me. We cut a Christmas tree out of a brown paper sack, decorated it, and stuck it on the shiny wall of our cabin with the presents on the floor beneath it.

On Friday December 22, Dick and I were in the cabin chatting with Mark and Steve when a message came blaring over the ship's loudspeakers: "Dick and Helen Griffin, please report immediately to the information desk." Eleven-year-old Philip, playing with some friends on the dock, had fallen backwards off a ten-foot ledge near the ship into rocks, mud, and oil. A big burly brother from Africa had jumped down and carried him out. He was in the ship's hospital. The gash was very deep, and the doctor from Singapore explained to us about the three layers of twelve stitches he was putting in Philip's head. An x-ray of his skull showed everything to be okay. The wound healed fine, and the doctor took the stitches out the following Friday before we left the ship. *He shall give His angels charge over thee!*

One of my Bible study groups met in the home of Betty Harder in the upper-class district of Lomas. She became ill, however, and her husband had her committed to a mental institution in the south of the city. Time went by, and none of us were allowed to visit her or have any contact at all, but we continued to pray for her.

Early one morning, after months of praying for Betty, I felt the Lord impress me with, *You can see her today.* I went straight to the phone to call her house, and a maid answered. "It's an amazing thing that you should call today," she said. "She has just been released from the hospital this very morning and will be here at the house but for just *one* hour. Then she flies to Houston and will not be coming back."

I drove straight there, astounded at God's timing. Betty came out of her room, and I watched as she moved like a zombie down the hallway to the living room to meet me, like death itself walking. We sat on the couch, and I prayed for her as the Lord had been putting in my heart to pray. A total change came over her, and when I said goodbye, it was to a different Betty. I left the house rejoicing at His healing and deliverance for her. That was 1979. I have not heard from her again.

I did talk to her husband, Jim, on the phone after that. I was able to give him a Scripture verse of promise that God had put on my heart for him.

He hung up with a "Humph." I never heard from him again but later was told that he died. *Lord, have mercy on us all.*

David and Miguel's mother and sister, who attended one of my Spanish Bible study groups, came knocking on the door. "Can you come help?" they pleaded. "There's a girl who is demonized, and no one has been able to help her. They've had pastors come and pray, but she has only gotten worse—violent and aggressive and trying to burn the house down."

"Wow, I don't know," I said. "I'll need to pray about it and talk to my husband." They agreed to return. I went to prayer, seeking God's wisdom and felt impressed that with Dick's consent and prayer covering I should go. So I called him at the bookstore and explained the problem. "If you've prayed and feel God wants you to go, then I would say yes," he said.

"Only if you're praying for me while I'm there," I replied, "because I can't do it; it's something God has to do." We had prayer over the phone, and he promised to be praying. I called Inez and Lupita and told them I would go. We descended an uneven, precarious dirt trail that reeked of pigsty. I paused at the doorway, observing women seated motionless on chairs, lining two walls of an otherwise empty room.

"Do all of you believe in the Lord Jesus Christ?" I asked. They all nodded. "Do you believe that by His blood He is able to set this girl free?" They acknowledged that they did. "Then you be praying as I go in." In the small room to my right lay a pretty young woman tied to a filthy mattress, flailing, shouting obscenities, trying to get free from the dirty strips that bound her arms and legs to the sides and foot of the bed frame.

As I stood there observing, I had the sensation of standing, actually standing in the blood of Jesus. That gave me confidence to begin. At first I didn't know how, not knowing how to name what was tormenting her. Then I knew what to do. As she was shrieking, I said, "You evil spirit that's saying *No quiero nada! No quiero nada!* I command you to come out in the name of Jesus and by His blood."

Immediately she lurched and became still, her head flung to the side. Then a few seconds later, she began screaming other words. I did the same thing, addressing the demon by what it was saying, and she spit up some yellow bile and was still again. This happened several times. Once I didn't understand the words and said "You who are saying that, I command you to come out in the name of Jesus."

After that she lay very still and opened her eyes. I said, "Jesus Christ has set you free. Do you believe in Him? Would you like to pray?" I prayed with her and for her and left her resting. Inez and Lupita told me later that a Christian family had taken her to their village and were caring for her. She was doing well. *There is power in the blood of Lamb.*

Halfway up to the border with our three boys later that summer, we stopped in Matehuala and checked into a motel. After long hours on the hot desert highway north, we were ready for a good night's sleep.

I was awakened at the crack of dawn, though, with the words very clear in my mind: "Hebrews 10:35."

What? I thought. *Hebrews 10:35? How is that? Who knows if Hebrews chapter 10 even has thirty-five verses? That's a lot of verses!*

Then equally as strong in my mind came, "Hebrews 10:35 and 36."

Thirty-five and *thirty-six?*

"Yes, and if you like, thirty-seven also—and there are more."

I quietly got out of bed so as not to awaken my husband and three sons, crept across the room, and found my Bible.

There in the still desert, mid-August morning, I read, *"Therefore, do not throw away your confidence, which has a great reward. For you have need of endurance, so that when you have done the will of God, you may receive what was promised"* (Hebrews 10:35-36 NASB).

These verses were timely. I did not know what was up ahead.

We were in Arkansas with Mother and Daddy in the summer of 1979, and my dad said some cutting and hurtful things to Philip. I fled Booneville thinking, I never want to go back there. If I do have to go back, I will never take my son, to subject him to that kind of treatment ever again.

But Philip and I had gone up to Tulsa with my sister Linda for a few days, when suddenly she announced, "Oh, I forgot! I promised Aunt Faye that you and I would decorate the cake for Ricky and Mona's wedding tomorrow."

I couldn't believe my ears. I had no intention of going back. I never wanted to go back ever again.

The next morning I shut myself in the bathroom and sat there crying. Linda came searching for me and knocked on the door. "Are you in there? Are you all right?" I let her in and sobbed out my problem.

She listened and said, "Let's pray for a miracle." That sounded strange, but I recognized I needed one. Right then she prayed and asked God for a miracle. Then she said, "I have an idea. You take Jody with you and head on down to Booneville. I'll come along later with Philip in my car."

Jody and I were driving along with the windows down and 150 miles of road ahead. As we merged left onto the Broken Arrow Expressway, suddenly the Lord spoke in my heart these words: *"All the times you have taught the women in your Bible studies in Mexico City about forgiveness—what about you? Aren't you going to forgive?"*

I'd never thought of that. It had not once entered my mind that forgiveness was in order. But I saw the truth immediately and said, *"Yes, Lord; of course, I forgive."* With that simple statement, all the bottled-up anguish inside of me sailed out through the open window, and I was totally free.

When I arrived at the back door, Daddy was standing there to welcome me with a big hug as though nothing had ever transpired—and it really was as though nothing ever had.

Thank You, Lord, for miracles.

After Ricky's wedding, the missionary I had met in Indore, India, Edna Brown, arrived in Booneville to visit. Mother told us about a newly formed group called *Abundant Living Fellowship* meeting in a home nearby. So Edna and I walked over there. They wanted to pray for me, and several of them had words of encouragement about Dick and me and the ministry in Mexico.

Afterward as we were just visiting, someone said, "I don't know if this is for you or not, but I will tell you, and you decide. I saw Satan with a huge pair of scissors. He was going to cut a relationship. I don't know what the relationship was, whether it was parent/child or what. But then I saw the Holy Spirit come and take away the scissors."

"Yes, I think that *is* for me," I said and told him briefly the miracle that had just happened with regard to my father and how it also related to my son—and therefore two different relationships: father/daughter, grandfather/grandson—and thanked him.

I didn't realize it then, but there was a third relationship in jeopardy that summer—that of mother and son. I had no clue how deeply wounded Philip was by me in this generational handout, even more than by his granddad.

Holy Spirit, thank You for coming, for taking away scissors, for healing wounds.

Time was drawing near for the 1979 Christmas campaign in Tijuana, but the touch of flu and its accompanying cough kept me awake at nights and left me feeling exhausted. That Friday evening Dick was getting ready to walk over to the weekly prayer meeting at the OM team house in Valle Dorado.

"I don't feel well," I told him. "I'm going to stay here and pray."

"That's all right," he said, pulling on his jacket and going out the door. "I'll send the girls over to pray with you."

In a few minutes they came traipsing through the front door. Rita came straight to where I sat, leaned over, and looked into my face. "Yes, you look awful!" she affirmed. "We're going to anoint you with oil and pray for you." Away she went to the kitchen for some cooking oil, which she slopped onto my forehead and began to pray. I was glad they were praying, and I joined in agreement. I wanted to be well, and I wanted to go on the campaign. I waited for the Lord to touch me, but nothing happened. I felt just as miserable as before.

I crawled into bed that night beside Dick and started coughing again. Oh no, I thought, not another miserable night of coughing and keeping Dick awake too.

Then I saw a light splashed overhead and in my spirit I heard the words, *"I have healed (I am healing you)."* A calm settled over me, and I lay very still pondering the words and wondering which He had said, "I *have* healed you" or "I *am* healing you" because I heard *both* but only one verb, both past perfect tense and present tense in only one word. He had already healed and was in the process of healing me. I fell asleep and did not cough again even once.

Thank you, Lord Jesus, for Your healing already done on the cross, already done as the girls prayed, already done as I received it, and being effectual in me. *The Great I AM heals you.*

One week later we left Mexico City with a busload of OMers on the forty-seven-hour drive across the desert stretches of northwestern Mexico to the border town of Tijuana, I reveled in the miracle of total well-being. Seeing headlights of oncoming vehicles in the darkness reminded me of the light over my bed, and I gave thanks. Seated there beside Dick, I read during the daylight hours the entire book, *I Dared to Call Him Father,* the story of a high-society Muslim woman in the Pakistani government who became a Christian.

It was an amazing story. On the day we arrived, Philip had me tell him the entire narrative without leaving out a single detail. He lay stretched out on his sleeping bag in our host's home on the outskirts of Tijuana, nursing a swollen eye and jaw from an aggressor's fist in an unjust punch that Friday at the American school. We put some medicine on the swelling, and I spent the day with him while Dick was out in early evangelism with the seventy-five Mexicans who had already arrived, and Steve was in San Diego shopping for sleeping bags.

After the whole story of the Pakistani lady, he wanted to hear more, so I told him another story I'd recently read and then got him interested in a crossword puzzle while I wrote a letter to my parents.

The next day we all went to San Diego to pick up Mark, now a senior at French Camp Academy. We'd gotten him a plane ticket to San Diego, and he was scheduled to arrive Tuesday evening at 6:55. Heavy fog caused his plane to divert to Los Angeles, however; so he caught a bus from there and arrived in San Diego at 3:00 a.m. Wednesday morning.

It was a good campaign for us as a family. Dick felt awkward, though, being the leader, and being placed out on the edge of town, out of the mainstream and out of touch with the teams. One night one of the teams showed the film, *Como Ladron en la Noche*, with the words of that haunting song, "Ain't no time to change your mind, the Son has come and you've been left behind." Philip dashed back to the room breathless and frightened. Right then he wanted to pray again and make sure he was prepared and not going to be left behind.

The Bennetts drove down from Los Angeles and invited us out for a meal. They had taken Philip into their home the six weeks we were in India the year before, and they had been sending support to us toward Philip's tuition at the American School so I could be freed up to teach Bible studies instead of continuing to teach at Greengates. *Thank you, Tom and Elizabeth!*

Chapter 4

The 1980s
My Dark Night of the Soul

"If we're going to be friends," the new lady in my Sunday school class said, "then it's your turn to come to my house."

I checked my calendar. "Tuesday, February 5 is a holiday," I replied. Normally I led two study groups that day—one in the Satelite area in Spanish and one in the Lomas area in English—but they would be suspended for the holiday. She drew me a map of how to get to her apartment. My little VW bounced along the dirt roads of the Navidad colony for the first time. What a change from downtown. Her directions were exact and landed me right at the red metal gate that opened into a patio with a pigsty on the left and a snarling dog named Magoo on the right. She showed me how to approach Magoo so he would not bite but would allow us to go up the stairs. That was my first day in Navidad, a working-class neighborhood on the southwest side of Mexico City.

"I have to go back to California in March," she later told me. "Can you come out and teach my Bible study while I'm away? Come to one of our meetings before I leave so you can meet the ladies." I loved the dear women in that group: Beatriz, Salud, Raquel, Malena, Consuelo, Petra, Maria Luisa, Marta, Julia, Mercedes, Carmen, Hilaria, and others.

When her time came to leave, she asked me to drive her to the airport and said, "I don't know if I'll be returning or not. My pastors want to talk to me, and they'll make a decision." She opened her Bible and read two verses as we traveled along the *Viaducto* and passed the hangars. She said they were for me, as though commissioning me.

> *And he said, The God of our fathers has appointed you to know His will and to see the Righteous One, and to hear an utterance from His mouth. For you will be a witness for Him to all men of what you have seen and heard.* (Acts 22:14-15 NASB)

It was sad seeing her go and thinking she might not be returning. It seemed I was always looking for a friend with whom to share spiritually; and every time a friendship was beginning, it was time for the person to move away.

She did show up again, though, but with a different agenda. She hinted that she had learned something while she was away. It turned out to be demons and deliverance. I had done some reading on the subject, one book in particular, *Deliver Us from*

Evil, by Don Basham, which I had used to pray for myself about anything in me that might hinder my walk with the Lord.

So when she brought up the subject after a meeting in English where I was invited to speak, I said, "I *am* free." She insisted I was not free, and she had made a list of things I needed to be freed from. So at her insistence I allowed her to pray against them and believed it to be all resolved.

On March 23 our team went to Chula Vista headquarters for Campus Crusade in Cuernavaca for the OM conference with Canadian directors Bert and Heather Kamphis, and my new friend went along. On the beautiful grounds of the conference center, we shared together along with all the other participants. But at the same conference where she made herself available as a friend to talk and pray together, she began to taunt and trouble me. She would slip from one mode to another. Displays of friendship alternating with accusations and unreality left me dismayed. She became obsessed with seeing demons everywhere and in everyone.

On the evening of Philip's thirteenth birthday, April 28, 1980, I was doing my reading in the Gospel of Matthew. *"If your right hand offend you, cut it off."* The verse stood out like a command for me to break off this relationship. It was not that she was my right hand, but she wanted to be that and more. She was a sick woman. She was pulling me down, and I was not able to help her. She had invited me to dine the next day at the classy revolving restaurant atop the Hotel Mexico on *Insurgentes Sur*. The evening prior I chose from our supply a thin leather Bible and dedicated it to her as a farewell gift, writing the verse from 1 Peter 1:22 in the flyleaf.

We sat eating at what is now the World Trade Center, seeing the surrounding city as the restaurant slowly turned. "Our friendship cannot continue," I told her, and I enumerated the reasons why. She was alarmed and incredulous, but I was direct with her. "When I counsel women who are in an unhealthy relationship, I tell them they must break it off. I am following the advice I give to others."

Back in my VW in the parking lot, after pleas of *How could I do this to her?* and *I was supposed to be her friend,* as though I had made a pact, she sat lifelessly slumped with the Bible, staring blankly, wordlessly, as in a dazed stupor. What was going on? I had never seen anything like this before. What I had thought would be a simple transaction turned into something apparently earth-shattering for her. My natural compassion must have kicked in, because I forgot, "Does it offend you? Cut it off." Instead, I started thinking, *Wow, if it means this much to her, I guess I should go ahead and be her friend for her sake. It's not that big of a deal for me.*

That was the worst mistake I ever made. It *was* a big deal, and in that moment I voluntarily sacrificed myself on the altar of her manipulative demands. She now had an upper hand. That afternoon she told me we were not going to the Tuesday afternoon group I taught for Carol Huerta and the director and teachers from her school. I would call them and have my assistant lead it. She needed the time to set me free from all the demons I had just named and needed deliverance from—which were actually the things I had mentioned *she* was doing and were my reasons for breaking off any relationship with her. *I had just given in to a master manipulator.*

Shortly after that, I was asked to be president of Aglow. I had been attending the monthly meetings and had been one of their speakers and enjoyed the group of women very much. I talked with Dick about it, and he encouraged me, so I told the committee I would accept. The lady, however, was very upset. "If you take that, all hell is going to break loose in your marriage." What an ominous prediction. Of course, I didn't want all hell to break loose in my marriage. Who does? So in the end, at her insistence, I declined, although in my spirit I grieved because I felt it was something the Lord had showed me I would be doing and it was something I very much wanted to do. I laid it on the altar of sacrifice, not because *He* asked me to but because she petulantly insisted.

Dick and I were preparing to leave for Mark's graduation from French Camp Academy, then take him with us to visit the New Jersey office and attend a wedding there, and then do a speaking tour in eastern Canada before returning for OM's recruiting conference in Akron, Ohio, the first week of June. I was standing in the doorway of her apartment to say goodbye. "While you are in Canada," she said, "you're going to have a mental breakdown. It's going to be better that way. God can accomplish his work faster instead of dragging it out over a long period of time."

I don't know what "god" she's talking about, I thought to myself, *but it's not my God and not His work.*

"No," I told her, "I am not going to have a breakdown. There is no history of mental illness in my family, and I refuse to accept it." She looked shocked. "You are going to pray for me right now," I said, as I turned to leave, "that God protect me from any such thing." I made her pray against it before I went on out the door.

My mother, my sister Linda, and her son Billy traveled with us to Mark's graduation. We stopped at the Knolls in Stuttgart, Arkansas, on May 16, on the way to Mississippi. That night their little daughter Christy had a bad dream and told it to everyone the next morning. "All these bad snakes were around me, and I was very scared. But Ms. Helen, she started spouting off at all those snakes, and they left." That was comforting to me in all my distress, because there had been times when God had allowed me to pray against something evil and I had seen Him at work.

Mark graduated at the top of his class and was also named "*Mr. FCA.*" He had been star running back on the football team, won a short-story writing contest for schools in the southern USA, and also received a track scholarship to study at Delta State University. His class had gone to New York City for their senior trip, so we were glad to have him along to be our guide around the "Big Apple."

The trip was a disaster for me, though. The lady, believing herself in charge of me now, didn't want to lose touch and wanted us to communicate by telepathy. I had refused outright. I knew nothing about that and wanted to know nothing. Still, there was something oppressive coming from her that I was continually battling. Crossing into Canada I gazed in amazement at the mighty, majestic Niagara Falls. As I observed the churning unrest of the water below, I thought sadly, *That's a picture of me*.

While we were in Canada that month, the Women's Aglow folded in Mexico City for lack of an incoming president. I grieved over the ministry I surrendered at her insistence. It was something God had given me, and I had missed Him.

Midway through the preaching tour, some close friends of OM loaned us a beautiful home on a green slope on the banks to the St. Lawrence River. It was a peaceful respite and a little bit of heaven in the midst of our busy itinerary. We came back down through New York State at the beginning of June and visited my friend Sylvia Green and her family. It was a renewing time, talking and praying together. "I see you as a warrior drug off the battlefield wounded and bleeding," she said, but she gave me great encouragement. The time with her was a highlight of the trip for me.

When we got to Akron for the June conference, Bob and Kathi Smith, who had worked with us in Mexico, hosted us in their home. Mark flew from there on June 5 back to French Camp to serve as a counselor for two weeks.

Dick and I were sleeping on a hide-a-bed in the basement. On the dark, stormy night of Thursday, June 5, I had a series of dreams. The first two showed me the lady's true colors and what I personally was up against. The third was the only real nightmare I have ever experienced in my life. I awoke in total panic, pouring sweat, frantic to get back into the stadium Dick and I had just fled from in the dream and rescue her. She had been left sitting there in a catatonic state, and doom was coming down on the place and everyone still in it.

When my panic subsided, I quietly reviewed the dreams in my mind. Then I asked the Lord to erase them—unless there was a reason for me to remember them. I fell asleep and had a fourth dream, where my attention was called to the power of God's Word. *I still recall every detail of each of the four dreams as vividly as I did that dark night.*

Dream #1:

Dick and I are in front of the steps going up to a large official building with tall columns, and I am speaking to a woman behind the counter of an information booth. She makes a slanderous remark, which causes me to respond with a mild rebuke. She retorts with derision, and out of her mouth spews foul, blasphemous words that stick to my face and distort it. I try to say JESUS to rebuke the evil, but my mouth won't move to pronounce His name.

Time goes by while I keep trying to say JESUS, but can't. I look at myself in the mirror and see my face totally misshapen. I put my hands on it, trying to make it take its form again, but it just squishes around like lifeless putty. Still looking in the mirror,

I take my fingers and try to make my lips form the name JESUS, but that doesn't work either.

Time passes, and later Dick and I are standing again in front of that building, this time about halfway up the stairway, and the wind is blowing across our faces. Suddenly a freezing wind blows through my mouth, leaving my teeth filed down. I realize then that I can speak, and I say JESUS! Dick says, "Don't just say JESUS. Say His complete name. Then I say, "THE LORD JESUS CHIRST, HE IS LORD OF ALL." My teeth are about half their original size, but that doesn't matter, because now I can speak again. I CAN SAY HIS NAME!

Dream # 2:

I enter from the outside into the backstage right wing of an ancient, elegant, dimly lit theater. It is intermission, the curtains are drawn, and the lady, seated in the background at the end of a long table, seems to be overseeing a queue of women I know in powder-blue dresses who are preparing to perform. Some are taking a turn, going out to dance in front of the packed audience. I carefully watch the line moving forward and the women going out in front of the curtained stage. The dancers are in full view from where I am standing. To my great alarm I watch as one of the women I know dances. Her dress, of its own power, begins moving down off her shoulders to reveal her breasts, and her skirt of itself rises up in the center to reveal her nakedness.

I look at the women standing in line, women I know by name from my Bible study groups. They seem unaware of what is going on. Then I look in shock at my own dress. Aghast, I see it is the exact same powder-blue design as all the others; and as I look, I notice that of its own accord one of the shoulders is starting to lower. Alarmed at what is happening and aware that the lady is watching, I turn and flee. I'M GETTING OUT OF HERE!

Dream #3:

Dick and I park the car and go into a wooded area to attend a special event. It's extremely difficult to get in, though. We have to get down on our bellies to squeeze under board fences and through twisted vines and crawl over fallen tree trunks and many other barriers blocking the way. Finally, after much difficulty, we arrive at an open-air stadium with wooden bleachers.

Off to my right on a small section of platform next to the bleachers sits the lady in a straight-back chair, her head hanging low, apparently in a daze. I walk up to her, but there is no response. I walk slowly around her, observing, wondering if I should speak. But since she seems to be in a stupor, I'm hesitant. It's been a long, long time since we've seen each other, and there are so many things we would talk about; but on second thought, I really don't want to rouse her and face all the hassle. So I walk over to the bleachers and leave her sitting there behind a hinged room divider.

I don't like it in here, I'm thinking as I sit down tentatively on the very edge of a lower rung of the bleachers. A performance is starting up on the wooden stage, but Dick has gone on through the stadium and is visible just outside the exit, standing against a wall beside the door frame. As the singing starts, I position myself facing the exit, with my feet ready to spring forward at the slightest indication of danger. I don't like the place at all, but I'm waiting to see what is so sinister about it. The group on the stage in cowboy outfits finishes a gospel song, and the girl in the group comments on how much the third stanza had meant to her. Turning to the leader, she says, "I'm so glad you had us sing the whole thing, especially verse 3." He looks at her with a fake grin and in an affected voice says, "Oh, you liked it, did you?" When she sees she is being mocked, she pulls a gun out of her holster and pretends to shoot at him. I watch as she fires five shots—all blanks. Suddenly, though, the next bullet is real, and he falls dead.

I spring from my place and flee through the exit door, beckoning Dick to follow as I rush past him. We dash across a semi-wooded area, where the ground is brown and bare. Glancing behind me, I can see two men in a Jeep bringing the dead body out of the stadium. Oh, no, I think to myself, they see us running and think we're fleeing because we're guilty. What shall we do? The trees are too sparse to hide us from view, and we can't outrun them, so we both plop down on the ground, thinking we'd be less likely to be seen lying flat. But the men in the Jeep pull up to where we are. One of them gets out and hands me a summons to appear in court, saying I was there and it was evident I was guilty of the crime or I wouldn't be trying to escape. They drive on, and Dick and

My Dark Night of the Soul

I continue working our way back to where we had initially come in. It gets steeper and more difficult, though, as we get back nearer the entrance. It gets so hard, in fact, that I have to reach ahead and grab onto something in front of me to pull myself forward, even to take one step more.

Finally, we make it to a turnstile. We pass through it into a large courtroom. I stand waiting to appear before the judge, and Dick stands nearby, next to a large column. I watch as a woman responds to the judge, her voice affected with a little girl twang, play-acting in front of him with girlish gestures, watching her own reflection in a mirror, very taken with herself. He can see right through her, I say to myself. She isn't deceiving him at all, but she thinks she is.

Then it is my turn. As I stand in place, I suddenly see a woman come through the doorway dressed in a beige suit with box hat to match. She looks very smart and self-assured. When she sees me, she thinks, Aha! This is the one I can shift the blame on to. I stand there before the judge, who is seated high up overhead, knowing that he knows the truth. When he asks me to speak for myself, I tell him in a few simple words exactly what happened in the stadium. "And I fled," I tell him, "because I hate violence." I can tell he is pleased with my answer, and the man sitting beside him is also pleased and nods with a slight smile dismissing me. I turn to Dick, and we start out the door.

As we get outside, great crowds of people are flooding from the stadium. It was a game, now over, and they are discussing the plays and the scores. I have a sudden realization that a great disaster is about to come upon the stadium and that everybody left inside there is doomed. How can they be discussing a mere game? Don't they know the end is about to come on all the people who are left back there? It is then I realize the lady is still in there, sitting in a catatonic stupor. With the greatest fear I have ever felt for anyone in my life, and in total panic, not knowing if I can make it in time, I say to Dick, "I'VE GOT TO GET BACK IN THERE AND GET HER OUT!"

In that instant I suddenly awoke from the nightmare in horror and in a cold sweat. I lay there in the basement bedroom beside Dick, trembling, listening to the rolls of thunder outside. I had never had a nightmare before and never anything so terrifying.

"Dear Lord," I prayed, *"I don't know about these three dreams I have just had. Sometimes dreams are meaningless, and when I wake up they've disappeared. I ask you, Lord, to erase these from my mind if there is no reason for me to remember them. If for some reason you want me to remember them, then let them still be there when I wake up."*

I reviewed them in my mind and then fell asleep to dream once more.

Dream #4:
I am at a large conference center with many rooms. The man in charge behind the front desk is a powerful personality like a Luis Palau/Wayne Meyers combination. As I come up to the desk, I notice my

laundry has been done and is waiting there for me. I can see the green and yellow folded sheets showing through the clear plastic. I don't want to take the laundry yet. I just want my purse and my Bible, which are in safekeeping, so I ask the gentleman for them. As he hands them to me, he says, "I'm just amazed at what's in there."

"What do you mean?" I ask. "You mean the money I have in my purse?" I remember I have about six hundred dollars in it.

"No," he says. "I'm talking about that Book. The power in that Book is just amazing." I look down at my burgundy Bible and switch my purse underneath it. The Bible should be on top.

As I walk through the large vestibule, I hold my Bible where I can see it, and I ponder the man's words. Yes, he's right, I say to myself, there is power in this Book! I keep glancing down at my Bible as I walk, wondering if other people passing by also notice it.

I keep on walking through many large meeting rooms and wide hallways. One group of women dressed in white uniforms stops me and asks if I would stay with their group and be their teacher. I don't feel it is the right time, and keep walking, meeting many groups of people as I go along but not committing myself to any of them. Then I come out at the far end of the place to a wide, beautiful expanse of sky and stand there drinking in the beauty and feeling the wonder.

END OF THE SET OF FOUR DREAMS

When I awoke the next morning, I remembered every detail of all four dreams, so I considered them to be significant and wrote them down. The first three gave me insight into what I was dealing with in this association with the lady. The fourth dream reinforced to me the power of the Word of God, our "sword of the Spirit."

For the Word of God is living and powerful, and sharper than any two-edged sword, piercing even to the division of soul and spirit, and of joints and marrow, and is a discerner of the thoughts and intents of the heart. And there is no creature hidden from His sight, but all things are naked and open to the eyes of Him to whom we must give account. (Hebrews 4:12-13)

* * *

While in the New Jersey office on our way to Germany, our charter flight was delayed; and we were placed in the home of the Hoffmans, board members of OM, who had already left for the conference. That evening Dick received a phone call from Greenville, Mississippi, that his mother had passed away. So he caught a quick flight down for her funeral. Later, I wished I had accompanied him, to be with him at the sad time of his mother's death, but I had got pulled away by the lady, who had somehow tagged along with our party.

The women leaders in Europe had invited me to be the speaker for the OM Wives' Conference the weekend before the general council began. They wanted to hear more about our recent challenges as a family with Dick losing his eye to cancer, Steve having heart surgery, and my losing the baby. So I used Psalm 103 as my theme for the weekend, on *Forget Not All His Benefits*.

> He pardons all your iniquities.
> He heals all your diseases.
> He redeems your life from the pit.
> He crowns you with loving kindness and compassion.
> He satisfies your years with good things.

Dick and I were hosted in a home there in Mosbach, Germany, and walked each day to the OM conferences in the picturesque village. One morning while getting ready to go over for the general council sessions, I lost one of my contact lenses. When the time came to walk over, I still had not found it. I said to Dick, "You go on ahead to the meeting. I will stay here till I find my lens and then catch up with you."

I searched and I searched, covering every inch of our room plus the path across the hall to the bathroom and back. It had to be there somewhere, and I had to find it—but I couldn't. Worn out with searching, and not having a pair of glasses for recourse, I was at a total loss. I gave up. I knelt down beside the bed to pray. That's all I would be able to do, just stay back and pray. As I knelt there, though, with my bare feet facing up, the thought came to me: *Look on the bottom of your foot.*

Why, yes! I looked, and to my amazement, there it was, flat and dry, stuck tight to the sole of my foot. I very carefully removed it, washed it, and put it in to soak and soften in the contact lens fluid. Afterward I put it back in, marveling that it was not damaged. To me it was nothing short of a miracle! *Somehow, down on my knees has always been a winning position.*

We had lived in Pirules four years. That seemed to be our maximum in one place because the landlord (or landlady as it was in this case) would raise the rent annually when the contract came up for renewal, and by the fourth year it was exorbitant. At that point we would opt to search for a more reasonably priced place.

We searched high and low. One day Dick found an advertisement for a house in a new development in the far northern reaches of Mexico City on the highway to Queretaro. Well, if we wanted to drive up to the States, we would already be on our way! To me it sounded like a barren desert, but because Dick asked me to, I made an appointment with the owner to meet her at the Ford dealership north of the city.

Before leaving the house in my little Volkswagen, I prayed, "Lord, if this is not the place for us, please block it, so we will know." I arrived at the Ford place on time and parked under the huge clock as she had indicated, but no one showed up. I waited over an hour and then turned around and headed home.

To my amazement as I headed back, there sat a huge logging truck, which had lost its cargo all across the northbound lanes of the highway, and traffic was backed up for miles. The potential landlady was literally blocked. Later in the afternoon she called, apologizing for missing the appointment and explaining why. "I can set another time to meet you and take you to see the house," she said.

"No, thank you," I said. "We've decided not to."

Dick really liked the idea of living out there way north of the city, but as it turned out the only good offer was in Navidad, all the way to the south. Greg and Connie, missionaries from California, were moving back to the States, and their house was to be available.

Moving was laborious, because the landlady in Pirules wanted us out the day the contract expired, and Greg and Connie with all their stuff would not be leaving for another week. We packed our furniture and belongings into their living-dining area almost to the ceiling and accepted Jerry and Vicky's gracious invitation to spend the intervening week with them.

I looked at our new house and grounds and said, "Lord, but I wanted a pretty place."

I felt Him say, "You're going to make it pretty."

The house was more or less okay, although pigs next door shook it by ramming into the side. The small back yard had been picked to death by Greg and Connie's chickens, and the huge front yard was a rocky wasteland with only a water cistern beside a small evergreen tree. We contacted a gardener, Melqueades, to lay sod in both the front and back, and soon we had green grass everywhere. I planted some white lilies I brought from the Pirules house, and they multiplied quickly below the kitchen window in front.

The boys wondered why we made the decision to move out to such a poor area of the city. Steve and Philip dubbed our dirt road "I-10" in ironic jest. The corner vacant lot was a trash heap of smelly garbage. It was hard for Philip being at the American school and riding the school bus home every day. He had the driver let him out at a faraway stop and walked from there.

Philip complained constantly, and there was plenty to complain about, especially the pigs next door slamming into the side of our house. One day I said, "Philip, this is not good. Let's do ourselves a favor. No more complaining. Not one single word." And he stopped. I don't remember hearing another word of complaint from him. What amazing willpower my young teenager had.

Those early months of 1981 a group of us trained at Mexico City's Union Church as counselors for the upcoming Billy Graham Campaign. Mexico reneged on allowing the evangelistic meetings in the 105,000-seat Olympic Stadium, and Billy Graham had to preach in the *Arena Mexico,* which held only 22,000. Great crowds listened from the streets, and there was no space for people to go forward and be met by a counselor. Those of us who trained as counselors had to remain in our sections and watch for those who stood at the invitation to receive Christ and make our way to them if we could. Actually the place was too packed for any movement, and no one stood in my section. I continued to be in such a valley spiritually, though, that I was glad I didn't have to counsel anyone, plagued as I was by a certain person's demoralizing demands and accusations.

Fellowship in the little church there with the Mexican believers was exceptional, though, and made up for any hardship. It was a totally alive group of worshipers who hungered for God, to know Him better and love Him more. They were rich in faith and love for one another. It often made me think of that verse in James: "Has not God chosen the poor of this world to be rich in faith?" (James 2:5b)

One day I went over by myself to clean up at the meeting place. As I pushed the mop, I was praying, "Lord, let me worship You." It had been a long time since I had used my prayer language. As I mopped I began to sing. It was a beautiful melody, but I didn't know what I was singing, so I asked the Lord to give the words in English.

Multiply the loaves and the fishes.
Multiply thy Word through me.
The world is starving for the Bread of Life to eat and live.
Multiply thy Word through me.

Magnify the name of Jesus,
May He be lifted up through me;
If He be lifted up, all men will be drawn unto Him,
Magnify His name through me.

Cast your every care on Jesus.

He's the One who cares for you.
On the cross He bore your sorrow, guilt, and grief, and shame,
In love He gave His life for you.

I told the lady about how the Lord had given me the song and started to sing it to her.

She stopped me. "No!" she said. "No one with as many demons as you have could have the Holy Spirit."

A group of us met every week early in 1982 at the home of group members Connie Hannum or Consuelo Boyle, with the lady leading. There I was, almost like a guard dog, watching out for the women. We would listen to praise music, sometimes sing along with it, read Scripture, share, and pray for each other.

One day Connie was "doing deliverance" on the lady, who had been teaching her how to do it. They were seated on a level of the living room slightly above where I was sitting on a couch. I heard Connie addressing a demon in her. "And what are you doing here?" she commanded.

"I was sent to Mexico to destroy a woman leader," she replied.

At those words an alarm went off in my gut, like a flashing red light, and a prompting in my spirit to take very careful note of what was to follow.

"And how do you propose to do that?" Connie demanded.

"Trap her in a sexual sin," came the reply.

"What kind of sexual sin?" Connie challenged.

"Any kind!"
"And if you fail?" Connie asked.
"Then I will do it through guilt."
"Surely, in vain the net is spread in the sight of any bird" (Prov.1:17).

One day I came out of Connie's house looking for my little Volkswagen, which I'd parked out front. I looked all around. What had happened to my car?

A great deluge of water had come down that morning while we were all inside. Aha! I looked down the hill in the direction of the recent flow. There sat my Bug a long block away on the grass in someone's front yard! I walked down the hill to it, circled it, looking for damages. What a miracle—not a single scratch. A man came out of the house and pointed to his car with a tiny, almost invisible scratch on it. "Your car did that to mine," he said, "and you have to pay me."

"No way!" I replied. "Instead of complaining, you should be giving thanks to God that nothing happened to either of our vehicles." I got in my car and drove away.

I was invited to speak at Easter time on board the MV/ Doulos in St Petersburg, Florida. My themes for the women's conference were (1) *Praying for My Family* and (2) *Forgiveness*.

I had chosen those two out of a list submitted to me. Cathy Hicks was also a speaker, as was Kay Arthur. The lady caught a flight up with up with

Connie Hannum and Alejandra Davila and signed up to visit the ship and attend the conferences.

The day I presented "Praying for my Family" all went well. I felt good about it. But when it was my turn to speak on forgiveness, I never before experienced the difficulty I confronted that day. The ship's conference room was packed to capacity with 350 women. The problem was to my right a few rows down, where the lady sat with a dark scowl that never left her face. Down the middle, though, up into the back rows, sat an older woman with a glowing face. I tried to fix my eyes on her as often as possible, but mostly I felt I was plowing, and it was rough. I was totally cast on Him and thankful I knew what God had put on my heart to say or I would have fallen flat.

Later I went up to the book exhibit on the deck. No one was up there. I wandered through the aisles of books, reviewing the talk and feeling like a failure. Suddenly a young girl appeared. "Aren't you the speaker who just gave the teaching on forgiveness?" she asked.

"Yes," I answered.

"Well, I just want to tell you it was an amazing presentation. All the women around in my whole section were weeping." She went on to describe what it meant to her personally,

Later, the older woman with the glowing face found me too. Her name was Violet Chamberlain. "God brought you all the way up from Mexico," she said, "to give that message. And He brought me all the way down here from Canada to hear it! I am forgiving my daughter. Things are going to be different now." She became a faithful prayer partner of ours from that day on.

I learned a lesson. When I think I'm a total flop may be the time God has used me the most.

Dick and I discussed the need for us to take some time off. After twenty-two years of living in Mexico, we needed to take a break, and we needed family time together and to be near our three sons as they adjusted to different schools in the States. Mark was a junior entering John Brown University in Siloam Springs, Arkansas; Steve had just finished three months active duty with the Air National Guard and was enrolling as a sophomore at Oklahoma State in Stillwater; and Philip, now a sophomore at Hale High School in Tulsa, played first-string tackle on the football team.

Dick sent me up early in August to check out possibilities. Philip and I drove to several places, investigating, but nothing opened up. When we arrived back in Tulsa, Linda said, "Why don't you live with us? We've got plenty of room. We bought this huge house because George's mother wanted to come live with us, but now she has returned to Baltimore." We accepted their gracious offer. Linda toured Russia with a group of nurses that October, and I got to fill in for her as homemaker, preparing some of the family's favorite dishes—Billy often requested peach cobbler!

We met a young family from India while attending Christian Chapel. We invited them over for a meal and put our map of India up on the dining room wall.

They were delighted. "We have been in your country for six months," they said, "and this is the first time we have been inside an American home." One day we invited Susie McMullin, founder of the Center for World Missions in Galena, Kansas, to come for dinner, and she brought several of her family with their keen interest in missions. Susie had built onto her own house a small apartment totally equipped to serve missionaries who were coming through. We often stopped in Galena in our travels to meet with the prayer group and receive this ministry from them.

Dick and I went down to Matamoros that December 1982 for a week of pre-campaign meetings. This was Dick's twenty-fifth Christmas campaign and our first time ever to spend Christmas together as a family outside of the campaigns. They were our family Christmas tradition.

Dick awakened visibly shaken from a nightmare that spring. "It was horrible," he said. "I don't even want to talk about it, it was so awful." He started to head out the bedroom door, but I called him back.

"Honey, maybe you could tell me so we can pray together about it." He turned with a hint of relief and agreed.

"Mark was in this car going through the mountains," he began. "Somebody else was driving and there were several guys in the car. The car skidded off the road and down the side of the mountain and Mark was killed." The pain in his words was too great.

"Let's pray," I said. " Let's bind the enemy in whatever designs he has on Mark's life, and pray for

God's protection over him. Sometimes God gives us a dream like that so we can pray."

That's what we did. We knelt by the bed and prayed against anything of the enemy coming against Mark, and we prayed for the Lord's care over him and those traveling in that car. We got up from our knees with peace in our hearts that God had taken care of it.

We discovered afterward that Mark had gone with a group of fellow students from John Brown University backpacking through the Ozark Mountains during their spring break. Their plan was to hike and be on foot the whole way. They came upon a highway, though, and who should be there but one of their classmates, a foreign student with his old used car. He had a reputation for fast driving and they had no interest in a ride, but he coaxed them all aboard. He sped around a curve and went into a skid, losing control. The car turned upside-down as it left the highway and was caught by a tree on the steep mountainside.

They all crawled out and stood looking at one another amazed. No one was hurt even a scratch. The car was totaled. They continued on their way, sweaty, soiled, and shaken, backpacks intact, without letting anybody know of their close call. We had later inquired, because of Dick's nightmare.

Thank You, dear God, for taking care of them all, and especially our Mark!

We finished our school year with our sons in the States and returned to the house in Navidad the summer of 1983. Telmex, the Mexican phone company, came and installed the telephone we had solicited two and a half years earlier. Dick was away at the time with the OM summer team in southern Mexico.

The lady stormed in that evening, furious, her neck glowing a deep bright red as she spit out rage with every word.

"Why was your phone installed before mine?" she demanded to know. "My application was put in a year before yours!" Then she said, "I know why! It's because demons in Dick are in league with the demons of the head man at the telephone company." She finished her tirade and stomped out the front door, where she had entered uninvited.

I sat where I was at the dining table and listened as the metal gate to the street slammed shut. I actually felt as though a herd of wild horses had stampeded through my house and left me trampled in the dust. I forced myself to stand. I trudged up the blue tile stairway.

Three of her pastors had come down from her sending church in California. I had tried to speak with them about some of the issues, but they, being in tune with her, could not hear my viewpoint.

"Lord," I prayed as I walked into the bedroom, "I'm angry and frustrated. This woman wants to destroy me—my mind, my marriage, my ministry." She had systematically targeted all of those during the three and a half years I had known her. As I prepared for bed, I continued spilling my heart to Him about the hurt of her searing ridicule, her false accusations, her out-and-out rejection of anything I tried to say to her, and the apathy of the pastors from California.

The house was quiet as I finished emptying out my anguish and finally rested my head on the pillow. I was wide awake. Suddenly there before me as on a screen appeared the image of a huge cauldron of boiling water with flames leaping all around. As I gazed at this flaming cauldron, I saw myself standing in the middle of the bubbling water. Somehow I knew I needed to respond. The Lord wanted a response from me to this.

Yes, I acknowledged, that's where I am right now. *It's a purifying process.*

When I did this, the picture changed. To my amazement I saw Jesus Himself standing there with me amid the flames in the boiling water. My heart swelled with gratitude and wonder. *"Lord, thank You! What more could I ask than to know that I am not alone in this, that You are taking it all with me."*

I thought that was a good ending. Just to know that He was in this with me made it somehow bearable; but as I continued to gaze at the picture, it changed again. I saw the two of us face each other, and we started to laugh. As I looked into His face and laughed with Him, all my anger and hurt and frustration of the day flowed out on the waves of laughter, falling over into the flames and vanishing. I sensed a profound relief.

I thought again that the picture was over, but to my surprise the scene changed once more in an astounding manner I could never have imagined. I began to merge into Jesus. I watched myself move inside of Him, something like a letter entering an envelope. I became enveloped totally inside Him, so that only He was visible. He stood there in the boiling water among the flames, but I was hidden inside Him, and *He was taking it all*. It was not even touching me.

I kept watching, marveling, as Jesus stood there alone, as I was hidden in Him. Then the flames gradually died down, the water got still, and the vision vanished. *In Him*. I had never before grasped so tangibly the truth of being *in Christ*. I lay there thinking of the words in Colossians 3:3, "Your life is hidden with Christ in God." I fell asleep, like a child tenderly enfolded, free from care, embracing the wonder of being *in Him*.

On awakening the next morning, I was still permeated with His peace and this extraordinary sensation of being in Christ. It was a busy day. My husband was returning with the OM team of thirty young people in time for dinner. I stood at the kitchen stove chopping zucchini for a vegetable soup when she entered again, Bible in hand.

"You are the false prophetess Jezebel," she declared, poking her finger at Revelation 2:20, "and you'll be cast on a bed of sickness together with all those who follow you."

I said nothing. I glanced at her standing there with her Bible open and kept on dicing the mound of green squash. The sensation of being in Christ was never so real to me. I was totally shielded and held secure, hidden away in Him.

"Here I have written down what God showed me," she declared, extracting a piece of paper. It seems that according to her, the local pastor Carlos had not experienced the deep things of Satan but I had. She pronounced another barrage of condemning words on me from the same chapter, jabbing her index finger at the page of her Bible.

Dear Lord Jesus, I prayed in my heart, *You are taking all of this.* I felt enclosed in Him. *If anything being said here is for me, let it come on through; otherwise You have taken it all.*

She finished her tirade, looked at me sideways, and then turned. I watched her slink out the front door.

In September 1984, Dick and I attended OM's fall conference in Belgium on the spacious grounds of the Belgian Bible Institute. Steve was traveling with a friend to Russia for the fall semester and stopped to see us in Belgium. In my free time, I read a book from the institute's library written by a German author, Dr. Kurt E. Koch, titled *Occult Bondage and Deliverance.* It confirmed a great number of things I had experienced in trying to relate to this person challenging me. I pondered them as I closed the book, sitting there under the tree on the green grass.

It had been three and a half years since I first determined to break free from her but was caught by her manipulation. Over this time I had known of a surety that God was with me, that for some reason I did not see He had me there, and that I was not to leave until He gave the go-ahead. That day, in

Belgium, unexpectedly, out of the blue, I felt Him say, "You are free to move now."

On our way back to Mexico, Dick and I stopped in the New Jersey office, where Dave and Cathy Hicks were now the area coordinators. I asked the three of them to pray for me, for the breaking of any bondage or oppression coming at me from this person.

That evening after we arrived back in Mexico, Dick headed across the city to the team house for the Friday night prayer meeting. He came back excited. "Guess what!" he said. "Samuel Zuñiga and his wife are moving temporarily to another city and offering us their beautiful home in the nearby Cuajimalpa neighborhood, almost rent free—for whatever we want to pay for it." I could hardly believe my ears. "Do you want to take it?" Dick asked.

"Oh, yes!" I said. "I certainly do want to take it!"

We moved into that lovely house with its huge back yard, gorgeous flowerbeds, and seven tall pine trees, plus hummingbirds! There the healing began. Every time I began to feel an oppression coming, I would tell Dick and ask him to pray with me. Even though I was out of the area, I felt like a watchdog on the side of a hill looking into the valley, vigilant for the women I had taught in Navidad.

Beatriz, who had not been well, became extremely sick. When I got news that she was near death, I felt a strong conviction that I should lay hands on her and pray. So I called her sister, Salud, who offered to bring her over. Beatriz arrived that day, flanked by Salud and the lady. The two bodyguards, stony and resistant, assisted Beatriz to the couch and sat snugly up against her on either side. As I looked at the situation, wondering how I was going to lay hands on her and pray, *knowing* that was what I needed do, the doorbell rang. While I was detained at the gate, singing in Spanish began in my living room: *"There is power, power, wonder-working power in the blood of the Lamb..."* The peculiar force with which it was being sung made me know that it was against me, and they were praying to ward me off. The lady was intending for Beatriz to die.

But I walked boldly back into my house and said in Spanish, *"I have invited Beatriz over to lay hands on her and pray for her healing."* They moved in even closer to her, but I went over and wormed my way in and put my arm around her and prayed for her protection from all evil and for God's healing.

She is still alive today in Navidad and teaching multitudes of women to know and follow the Lord Jesus Christ.

"Why did you hang in there so long?" many people have asked me.
- Once I was trapped, I knew I was not to try to change it myself but wait for God to do it. For some reason I could not discern, He had me there and I was to commit myself to Him in the midst of it. I had the overriding conviction He was in it and with me in it.
- I wanted to discern what truth, if any, could be gleaned from what she taught. Did it work out in reality? Did it produce in the end good fruit or bad? I wanted to watch and see. Many

of the things she taught were good and true. But they too soon became mixed with harshness and vengeance toward those who did not submit, and the brew was lethal. *"But the wisdom that is from above is first pure, then peaceable, gentle and willing to yield, full of mercy and good fruits, without partiality and without hypocrisy" (James 3:17).*

- All the while I waited and expected Him to vindicate me, as I continually "committed *myself* to Him who judges righteously," as it says of *Christ* in 1 Peter 2:23. Of course, He, the sinless, righteous One, is clear of all false accusations, while I, still in this body, have sin to deal with on a daily basis. I have nothing to defend me but the blood of Christ, and by it I am already vindicated, cleared of charges made by the enemy of my soul from things Christ has already died to pay for by His death, by His blood alone, His righteousness alone. I learned that I need not seek more vindication than that.
- My eyes don't see here a world of things going on behind the scenes, of forces maneuvering the puppet strings of souls in bondage to the darkness because they refused the light offered them. I had compassion for her, wanting her to be saved out of it. My attempts, however, were met with outright rejection. When I told her about the nightmare and my panic to rescue her from the doom about to descend, she challenged me: "Well! What did

you do about it?" I told her what I had done in attempting to communicate it to her. "Then when you would not listen, I wrote you a letter and you burnt it." She did not respond.
- I had to accept that only when standing before God who knows all things would I know and understand. Only in His presence will we be seen for what we really are. Truth will reign there. The distortions and twisted truth are going to be untwisted and reality is going to be recognized.

Shortly before we moved into the house in Cuajimalpa, my brother-in-law, George Wiland, came to spend two weeks with us. An old white car that pulled strange and dangerous tricks had been donated. One day Dick was driving along a busy highway when all of a sudden the hood flew up and covered the windshield, totally blocking his view! God's mercy saved him from a terrible accident.

Dick made sure the problem was corrected before we left with George for the annual spiritual life conference in Valsequillo, Puebla. On our way, though, just as we approached a busy intersection in the south of Mexico City, the brakes suddenly went out!

"Lord," I screamed, "Save us!"

People must have known we were going to be barreling through without stopping because each vehicle in the crossfire wove from the left and from the right as though choreographed as we sailed through.

I named that deceptive car "The Whited Sepulcher," and we got rid of that death trap after that trip.

I went up to San Luis Postosí early to give a pre-campaign seminar for the women while Don Hamman did three days of pastors' conferences. I returned to our lovely house in Cuajimalpa to welcome family and guests as they arrived. Ruth Eaves came from Arizona and went on up to San Luis Potosi for the campaign. Mark brought Terry Sprouse, a classmate from OSU, and they went on up to the campaign too. This was the first Christmas in many years we did not have hundreds of college students arriving from the U. S and Canada to join us. It was a first all-Mexican campaign!

The day Philip arrived from Tulsa, in December of 1984, I was alone at the house, preparing to drive to the airport in my little VW to meet him—but I couldn't find my car key! I searched everywhere, high and low, but to no avail. The key was not to be found. I could not leave Philip stranded at the airport. Those were still the days of no cell phones or lines of communication to let a person know what was happening. And I had no one to call on.
Desperately I prayed, "Lord, help me!"
A thought came to try one of the keys that belonged to our book storage shelves at church. Maybe one of the three would fit the ignition. What a wild idea, I reasoned. Anyhow, where were they? Those keys were relics from years back when Dick

and I managed the literature exhibit at church. If I were to find them, it seemed preposterous to think one would fit the ignition of a car.

But somehow I found them. I tried the first one—nope. Neither did the second one work. Then, to my surprise and delight, the third one started the engine! Away I sailed, singing across the city, to get Philip!

Philip and I had Christmas dinner together. When the campaign finished, the house filled up with our sons and our guests getting ready to welcome Steve back from Russia, where he had been studying at the Pushkin Institute in Moscow for four months. He arrived to a joyful, welcome-home turkey dinner on New Year's Eve around the family dining table.

Back in the late 1970s I'd had a dream about Steve. It didn't scare me because I didn't take it to be prophetic; rather, I received it as an assurance concerning something that had often bothered me. I had noticed that the times I experienced real fear always had to do with something happening to one of my children. For example, when Miguel up the street smashed his fist into Steve's glasses and got slivers in Steve's eye, fear swept over me when I heard the news, and I had to coax Steve out of his hiding place under the couch to discover if he was all right.

Another time that fear gripped me was in April of 1977 when Dr. William Daniel in Booneville, Arkansas, called me into his office after doing Steve's physical check-up for French Camp, saying he had found a problem and Steve should see a heart specialist immediately upon returning to Mexico. Fear gripped me then for my child. In both cases Steve turned out all right—Miguel's mom had carefully removed the splinters of glass from Steve's eye, and in Mexico City some of the best heart specialists in the world discovered and removed the blockage in the aorta artery of Steve's heart, and his problem was corrected.

My troubling thought was this: If I experience a gripping fear when something threatens one of my children, how would I react if something really bad happened to one of them? How would I handle it? Could I handle it? Would I fall apart?

This is the dream I had.

I was walking up a long, lonely stretch of highway with green mountains all around. I knew as I walked that there had been an accident up ahead and that Steve was involved, that fifty-six people had died when two buses collided. So I was not surprised when I saw in the distance two men in uniform standing beside the highway waiting for me.

"There has been an accident," they said, "and there were no survivors. Your son was on one of those buses."

As I stood facing the two men, I realized in a split second that I had the power to choose how I would react. I raised my right hand in the air in front of them and said, "May Jesus Christ be praised."

Shortly after that I shared the dream with my friend Loella Scarpa. "I'm not scared by the dream," I said. "I feel like God gave it to show me that even in the worst thing imaginable I would be able to choose my reaction instead of coming apart and not being able to handle it."

Many years went by, and I hardly had occasion to think of the dream again. In 1984 Steve went off to Moscow for his fall semester of Russian studies at the Pushkin Institute. This was his first time abroad, and we were all excited for his opportunity to study in another country. His Russian accent was so good that people even took him to be a Russian from the Baltic Coast.

"Steve, when you're in Russia, please keep a journal," I said. "It would be valuable to you, and I'd like to read about your experiences while you're over there." Steve wrote letters home to us, telling about his studies and his travels, giving us his schedules of classes and trips. He traveled often by train with his classmates, visiting other parts of the USSR.

Then on December 2, 1984, I woke up with a strong impression: *This is the day of the dream. Pray.* So all that morning I did. I prayed as I went about my duties, and I prayed as I sat by the little gas heater in the Zuñigas' house there in Cuajimalpa.

I didn't doubt that I was supposed to be praying, but I thought, Steve is not traveling by bus. All his travels are by train. But I continued praying for him and those traveling with him. The morning passed. Then at 2:00 p.m. I had an equally strong impression: *Everything is all right now. You can stop praying.*

January 1, 1985. Almost a month had gone by since I prayed about the dream. Steve had arrived home on New Year's Eve, but there had been no opportunity to ask if he had kept a journal. I was curious about that day.

After breakfast Dick said to the boys, "Why don't I take you all bowling?" Everyone jumped to the idea. As they headed out the front door, Steve suddenly turned around and began rummaging through his duffel bag. "Hey, Mom," he said, "here's that journal you asked me to keep. It'll give you something to read while we're out."

The door had no sooner shut than I hurried to open up the carefully written pages to his December 2 entry. In amazement I read of their bus trip to another city, all sixteen students of his group—their day there, their bus ride home, the Christmas carols they sang. Steve also wrote that his roommate got drunk and threw up all over the bus and the bus driver made the roommate clean it up. Interesting. In a way I felt myself having been there, because I had been interceding for them on their whole trip. The most astounding part for me was the hour he noted they had arrived back at their dorm, 11:00 p.m. Moscow is nine hours ahead of Mexico City, so that was 2:00 p.m. Mexico time, the exact hour I was told, *Everything is all right now. You can stop praying.*

May Jesus Christ be praised!

Mexico's killer earthquake occurred on September 19, 1985. I grabbed the shower curtain for balance and avoided being flung against the mirror on the wall. "Wow, it's an earthquake!" I yelled. Since we'd lived out southwest of the city, there had been many tremors in the center we hadn't felt at all. So I exclaimed, "If it's this strong out here, what must it be like downtown?"

We had no idea. Power was off. Telephone lines were down. We headed on over to the Cuajimalpa church with Dave Hicks, who had come down from the New Jersey office. Enrique Sandoval broke into our last session of the morning with news of the terrible devastation downtown. He had managed to get to us in his car, but the earthquake had destroyed a great part of the city.

"What about the Continental Hotel, where we're having the pastors' breakfast tomorrow morning?" Dick asked.

"Half of it has caved in," Enrique said. Dick found that hard to accept and with his usual "mountain challenging" attitude wondered if we couldn't go ahead and meet in the part that hadn't fallen!

We went back to the house and listened in on Enrique's battery-powered radio. I couldn't believe my ears. The newscaster read a list of the buildings that were still standing. What! Were the ones that fell too many to name? Apparently so. Mexico City had suffered a devastating earthquake. All the world was hearing it had happened, but nobody could get any news from us because all our communication lines were down. The next day there was another, almost equally strong earthquake, called an aftershock. We grieved for the people downtown who were doubly stricken and traumatized with this second one.

Dave Hicks was able to change his ticket to leave Saturday from the airport. I stayed up late writing a letter for him to mail from the States when he flew back on Saturday. At least our family and friends would get a letter from us saying we were safe.

After the earthquake, the lady received funds from her church in California to do relief work downtown. When she had fulfilled that commission, her pastors came and took her back with them.

When the Christmas campaign ended, Darrel and Kathy Grasman, OM Mexico leaders-in-training, invited us to go with them for a couple days to the resort town of Oaxtepec, our family's favorite vacation spot! We loaded into Darrel's light blue van with a white grill on the front. Dick rode up front, while Darrel drove. Kathy and I sat right behind them with little Julie and Krista. Mark and Philip were in the back.

The day ended, and late December's early sunset settled darkness over the magnificent mountains. We sailed along the modern four-lane toll highway toward Cuernavaca. Dick and Darrel conversed, and Kathy and I chatted. Suddenly, without warning, Kathy screamed, "Darrel, stop!" Nothing at all was visible up ahead, just dense blackness beyond the beam of our headlights.

Darrel threw on the brakes, and we screeched to a halt just in time. We had almost crashed into a huge bus straddling the highway, its nose jutting into the center meridian. Its long body totally blocked our lane. If Kathy had not screamed, we would have driven straight into it broadside.

"Kathy!" I said, "Not one of us could see that! How did you know to scream 'stop'?"

"I just felt danger up ahead," she responded, "and I had to make Darrel stop."

We all marveled. We gave thanks to God. We continued to our destination and enjoyed adjoining rooms at Hotel Tepoxteco on the beautiful grounds and gardens of Oaxtepec, where Hernando Cortez and his men from Spain had lingered and relished the beauty en route to Cuernavaca during their conquest of Mexico in 1521.

About a month later, Dick and I arrived in Tulsa at the Wilands' house on 21st Place. To my surprise Linda began telling me with great pain about a horrible nightmare she had had about a month before.

"In my dream I saw you traveling in a light blue van with some kind of white grating on the front," she said to me. "You were going along a mountain highway with gorgeous scenery, much like in western Arkansas where we were born. Suddenly there was a terrible accident. I didn't know what caused it. I couldn't see; but I woke up screaming and crying out because you and Mark were both killed, and Dick was in serious condition in the hospital.

"An overwhelming anger came over me," Linda said, "for the stupid thing that caused the accident. I couldn't see what that thing was, but the anger was so strong I could hardly stand it." She began to cry out to God for us.

"Linda, I can tell you what happened," I said, and I related to her all the details of that dark night on the mountain highway. God must have used her dream, and her crying out to Him, to save us. *Linda screamed and cried out to God. Kathy screamed and cried out in warning to Darrel. Praise be to God for His deliverance!*

In October of 1986, after we had lived in Cuajimalpa two years, the Zuñigas were reassigned to Mexico City and needed their house back.

We had served in the Cuajimalpa church those two years, Dick as an elder, and I teaching the ladies' Sunday school class and their weekly meeting. Some of the ladies were open and eager to learn from the Lord, but nothing like the ones in Navidad. I could count on three fingers the women who were open and responsive to the Lord—Alma, Felicitas, and Lulu. None of the other women, even wives of the head leaders, had shown spiritual growth. In fact, one Sunday evening while teaching the parable of the sower from Mark 4, I asked them to draw on their homework sheet the four types of soil in the squares indicated. Everyone did that as we discussed the meaning of the parable. Then as an application, I asked, "Which type of soil are you?"

One of the leader's wives shouted, "You have no right to ask us that! I am not going to answer!" I had offered the question for personal examination and sharing. As she sat there with her arms folded, I could almost see the birds of the parable diving down, snatching away the seed, lest it take root and grow.

After two years in the Zuñigas' house and at the neighborhood church, we told the leaders we would be moving. Carlos and Raquel, pastors in the Navidad church, wanted desperately for us to return there. Raquel even found an apartment and begged us to consider it. We finally did and became active in the church again.

Steve was going to surprise Stella with her engagement ring at Christmas when we were together in Booneville, but he surprised her with it on his birthday November 30. Mark's commitment in Botswana as a Peace Corps volunteer was to go through May of 1988, so he wouldn't make it for their August 1987 wedding.

I flew up to Tulsa on December 10 from Mexico City; Philip flew up December 19 from Arizona, Dick on December 22 from Mexico City, and Steve and Stella down from Montreal on December 23. Then we all headed to Booneville. It had been nineteen years since I'd been with Mother and Daddy in their home for Christmas. Mother lost her voice, but nevertheless was able to communicate her love and caring to her brood, who converged there.

Carlos and Raquel, pastors in the Navidad church, liked for us to plan conferences together, do evangelism with the church, have meals with them, and even go to the track to work out. We started going early of a morning to do some laps. On the morning of April 3, 1987, we finished at the far corner and were crossing the field back toward the house. I walked toward the basketball court and jumped, thinking the ledge was just a stair-step high, as it was at the other end, but to my surprise in that particular place it was quite a tall embankment.

During that split second in the air I thought to myself, *I'll have to land on my feet.* Under normal circumstances that may have worked out, but my left knee had been weakened the week before by a blow against a rock while climbing a mountain near Popocatepetl; so my left foot turned outward when I landed. I looked down aghast at the backwards "L" it made. Raquel dashed to me, grabbed my foot in both her hands and popped it back into place. Then she said a quick prayer that I not have pain, and then Dick and Carlos lifted me completely off my feet and carried me to our vehicle. It was humiliating to be carried. I had always been the independent one.

Amazingly, I had no pain that whole day at the ABC Hospital, waiting for bone specialists to be called in and getting prepared for surgery. God had answered Raquel's prayer.

That evening I had surgery to repair four fractures in my left ankle. I felt like lumber on a workbench as they hammered and inserted metal screws and plaques into the bones, but I felt no pain because of the local anesthesia.

On his first house call, my doctor asked me when had I first experienced pain. "After you operated on it!" I said, and we both laughed, as though it were his fault.

When I went for an appointment later at his office, he was pleased with the progress and said with admiration, "You have a very strong spirit."

Later when I reported to Dick what the surgeon said, he asked, "Did you tell him what Spirit it is?" I was sorry that I hadn't. Dick should have been in there with me. He would have told him. He never misses an opportunity.

I was still on crutches, standing outside before going in to the meeting that Sunday morning when the lady suddenly arrived. She and three of the pastors had come back for a visit.

"*You* come here?" she asked in shocked disapproval.

"Here I am," I replied, stating the obvious.

During the service, though, she gave some words in Spanish in a prophetic tone of voice, speaking as though God Himself were speaking, saying, "I am controlling everything." She spoke of how God was going to come in judgment with a rod of iron and the sheep were going to be scattered, and offered other dark predictions. I prayed as she spoke that the congregation would be protected and not understand or be affected by what she was saying.

The four of them were there several days and came to our apartment for visits and even invited us out to eat the last evening. Everything was friendly and amiable, talking about how things were going and decisions that were being made and how we would be cooperating.

It was a painful experience, therefore, the next morning before they all left for the airport to be told I was not to attend the church anymore. If my husband was invited to preach, then I could accompany him. Since they were taking her back to California and she could not attend, then neither could I.

I felt demolished inside as though a bombshell had hit. Dick took me for a long drive in the country, and I poured out all my hurt into his ears. He had been present for all the proceedings with the pastors, and he helped me see how they were influenced. My place was to forgive them and turn it loose. That was a liberating, life-giving moment when I did. I experienced again the miracle of forgiveness and how freeing it is!

Steve and Stella were married on August 15, 1987. Bishop Hollis of Montreal performed the ceremony. Stella was beautiful in her mother's wedding gown. After the wedding Dick was behaving strangely at the Montreal airport, trying to block me from going to certain areas, looking sheepish. I was puzzled. "What's going on?" I said. "What are you up to?" Then I spotted them—Steve and Stella—trying to hide behind some plants next to a big column. Dick knew, but it was supposed to be a surprise for me that we all four were on the same flight to Mexico. They were flying down for their honeymoon! I was so happy that Stella invited me to sit with her and share heart to heart for a great part of the trip.

Philip came down for his four weeks' Christmas vacation from school, and Steve and Stella came for three weeks. Mark was still in Botswana teaching with the Peace Corps and had developed a plan to put together a library before he left in May. We gave all our friends his school's mailing address, so large quantities of used textbooks began reaching him in time to get it set up.

The M/V *Logos* ran aground off the southern coast of Chile on January 4, 1988, but all 141 on board were brought safely to land. The ship still sits there today, a stark warning to other vessels going through those dangerous waters. Dick and I visited YWAM's ship *Anastasis* with Isaias and Oli Medel right after that to receive treatment for Isaias's eye. The directors of the YWAM ship welcomed us aboard and were especially anxious to hear any details of the cause of the shipwreck so they could be better prepared themselves when facing such dangers.

Later that year when our second year's contract on the apartment was almost up, our landlord, Bonfilio, said, "I'm going up on your rent."

"How much?" Dick asked. The landlord named the amount. "What? Why so high?"

"Because your neighbors on the third floor have not paid their rent. I have to go up to cover for my loss." That was our signal to move instead of getting our rent doubled to pay a wayward neighbor's debt. Darrel and Kathy wanted us to stay in the area because they had rented a nice little house not far from us. They searched for something for us in Contadera going toward Toluca.

Dick, however, felt that it was time to move out of the huge metropolis, the biggest in the world, his home for twenty-eight years, to a nearby smaller city. He also wanted to grant Darrel the freedom to operate on his own as director of OM Mexico instead of having the former director right at hand. Moreover, he longed to get away from the traffic and pollution to a smaller place.

For me, I was hungering for green. We had lived so long surrounded by colorless cement and pavement that I actually felt starved for green around me. Our apartment building had one lone rosebush, and I thanked God for it. The year before on the first day of December, I had gone with Kathy Grasman and Donna McGrath to Amecameca, where we cut down our own Christmas trees. I picked mine out, sawed it down, and decorated it in our little apartment for our family's celebration. It was beautiful and smelled wonderful, but it didn't last, and I was starving for green.

We had friends checking for a house for us in surrounding cities. Dick felt a drawing toward Toluca and began to go searching out possibilities there. However, each time he found a place that he liked and would start to come to an agreement on it, the door would close. This whole process was taking up time. Our contract would expire that Thursday, our deadline for moving out, and we had no place to go.

When Dick left that morning I knelt by our bed, where I would often kneel to pray. I was weighed down by the pressure on us, the time-running-out feeling. But most of all, the nowhere to go, no place to live, "where am I going to be?" made me feel desolate.

My Dark Night of the Soul

"Dear Lord," I prayed, "I don't like this feeling of not having a house. I've never had this feeling before of no place to be. I don't like it."

As I knelt there, I felt the Lord say to me, *I am your house.*

That was a new thought. I had never before thought of Jesus as a house, but as I meditated on it, I imagined Him being glorious walls that surrounded me, adorned with all the most beautiful things I could ever desire in a house. I felt so secure and special in my new house, Jesus Himself. I enjoyed imagining Him as every precious stone and colorful gem of every hue adorning the walls around me.

That evening Dick came back to the apartment elated. He had found the right place. He was going in the morning to sign the contract, but the next day at noon he walked back through the door crestfallen. "They changed the price on me, so I didn't sign. I can't do business with people like that." I understood and agreed.

"Pack me a lunch," he said. "I'm going to catch a bus, and I'll stay in Toluca until I find a place." I made him a sandwich and put a banana in the sack with it.

Then I said, "Have you called Rosa Leticia? She was going to be looking for a house in Cuernavaca. Maybe you should check with her before you leave." He dialed her number.

"Oh, yes!" Rosa Leticia said. "We've found several nice houses, and within your price range. Why don't you come? We can show them to you!"

So I made another sandwich and dropped in another banana, and we both hopped into my red car and headed south to the "City of Eternal Springtime."

I had made a list some time before of what I would like to have in a house. The first house we saw had everything on my list: a huge front yard with green grass and plants and flowers, three bedrooms for receiving lots of company, big windows letting in light, clean walls and floors, connections for my washer and dryer, and even a bathtub!

By five o'clock that same afternoon, we had signed the contract and were headed back to Mexico City to pack up and move.

Thank You, Lord Jesus. You give us Yourself, and You give us the desires of our heart.

"He who spared not His own Son, but delivered Him up for us all, how shall He not also with Him freely give us all things?"(Rom. 8:32).

The dear people from the Navidad church, along with some of our neighbors, helped me pack up, and Carlos and Raquel got a truck and helped us move. My love for the people of Navidad was similar to my love for those in India. They were poor but rich in faith. Out of their poverty they gave. They gave freely their time and their love. I would miss them.

After Carlos and Raquel helped us get moved in, we discovered it was their wedding anniversary! "Do you know any places to eat?" I asked Carlos. "Let us take you two out to celebrate!"

Carlos got behind the wheel and maneuvered us through the "eternal circles" of downtown

Cuernavaca to a VIPS restaurant. The manicured garden with its grass, trees, flowers, fountains, and green ivy climbing the stone walls imparted life to my hungry soul. As we dined and rejoiced with our friends in their happy marriage, I drank in all the delights around me of the fragrance, colors, fresh air, and music of the splashing fountains. *Thank You, Lord, for green pastures and for restoring our souls.*

Dick and I flew to Tulsa, spent Christmas with all the family in Booneville, and then headed up to Columbia, Missouri, for Philip and Deanna's wedding on December 30, 1988. Mother and Daddy observed the snow and ice still covering the ground and did not feel secure about making the trip. Deanna had decorated the church with candelabra and red poinsettias galore, which matched her attendants' dresses. She was radiant in her white gown, and her darling three-year-old daughter Jessica stole the show when it was her turn to enter, running jubilantly down the aisle, shoving one hand into Deanna's and the other into Philip's and attempting a somersault in the air!

In January 1989 we made our first trip to Puerto Rico. "Do the birds sing at night here in Puerto Rico?" I asked Luisa. It was dark outside the Paezs' cottage, and I listened with pleasure to the happy music. I had never heard birds sing at night.

Luisa laughed. "Those aren't birds," she said. "They're *cantaranas*—singing frogs! Puerto Rico is famous for them."

Thus began a delightful trip around a fascinating tropical island.

"Shake them out of their island mentality," Frank Dietz had said, as he commissioned us. "Challenge them with the needs in the rest of the world."

That's what we did, as we traveled around the island, speaking to different churches and groups. A highlight for me was being with the Tillotsons, in their home and in their church, and going out with her in evangelism at the doors, as she and I had done together in 1959 in Monterrey on my very first Christmas campaign almost thirty years before! She was already a seasoned missionary when I met her then, and now again I was blessed by her zeal to tell everyone about Jesus and invite them to a living faith in Him.

I enjoyed my meetings with women, both in the churches and outside at relaxed gatherings. I didn't go prepared with messages to give, so whenever I found out I had another meeting I would find a place to get alone and pray and seek God for His message for that particular group. On my knees—that is were I got them that trip.

"What's Puerto Rico like?" Mark asked me later.

"Well, if you look at the highways and the supermarkets, you'd think you're in the States. But the people speak Spanish!

Our first Christmas Eve in Cuernavaca in 1989 fell on a Sunday. We had our normal 5:00 p.m. meeting, and Miriam's mom and her aunt Josefina made tamales. Delicious! Since none of our kids were coming home and the Renz family, also missionaries, had three sons away in the States, I invited Buck and Lisa with their daughter Tabi for Christmas dinner on Monday. I also invited Bertha Veneberg, a little A/G missionary who was all alone.

I got the turkey in the oven early and was putting finishing touches on the meal when Benjamin and Gaby and their two children and Benjamin's parents from Mexico City arrived. Panic! Where was I going to seat everybody? But they graciously declined our invitation since they'd had their big family festive meal at midnight and were just paying a friendly call.

Since our family tradition had always been OM campaigns at Christmas, I was not so familiar with this custom of the big festive meal at midnight on Christmas Eve and a laid-back informal calling on friends on Christmas Day.

After dinner we enjoyed a game of "Reunion." Fun!

Over Christmas we kept "Gorby," the neighbors' gorgeous, golden cocker spaniel, while they were away. The day after Christmas he pulled my clean clothes down off the line and I had to give him a little spanking. The neighbors brought back a bottle of *Tequila* for us, a token of their appreciation. Benjamin offered to take it but he looked too eager, so I thought not. It went down the drain—the way my mother used to dispose of such. I guess I inherited her loathing for strong drink.

* * *

Chapter 5

The 1990s
"The City of Eternal Springtime"

When Mark and Joy married on June 2, 1990, all three of our sons had married within a three-year period. Joy had ordered small flowers, but the large colorful flowers that got delivered were a perfect complement for her and all her attendants in the Oklahoma City nature park. Mother and Daddy were able to be there, making it complete for me.

In September, for my fiftieth birthday, I asked Philip and Deanna's permission to take my little granddaughter Jessica on a road trip with me. We left Texas for Arkansas, Missouri, and Oklahoma, visiting family and enjoying our eleven days together. On Sunday morning we drove in the rain from Booneville to Buddy and Rosie's house in Eureka Springs, singing the whole way. We went with them to their Assembly of God Church in Berryville. I left Jessica in the class for five-year-olds and was sitting in the service with Buddy and Rosie.

At the end of the message, Pastor Keith Butler invited all the congregation to come kneel at the altar to pray. Since not everyone could fit at the long curving altar, some of us filled up the first few rows of pews. I was squeezed in with Buddy and Rosie in the second or third row on the left. In the midst of a time of prayer and worshipful singing in the Spirit, everything suddenly grew quiet as a woman kneeling at the altar around on the far right began to give a message in tongues. I paid careful attention, trying to pick out any speech patterns. As I listened, I thought, *I don't have the slightest idea what she is saying.*

As soon as I acknowledged that, a picture sprang into my mind of a great fire reaching all the way into the sky. The people who had gathered around it looked so tiny in comparison as they gazed upward, dumbfounded, not knowing what to do. When I realized this must be the interpretation, I felt nervous—this had never happened to me before. Then words seemed to appear beneath the scene like a caption: "The fire is not for your destruction but for your purification. Submit to Me, and I will bring good to you from it." Oh, no! I thought. This really is the interpretation, and I am probably supposed to say it.

I was more nervous than ever and wanted to stay put, but the thought suddenly came, *If you don't stand up and speak, the message will be lost.* So I stood and with a tremor in my voice spoke the words and sat back down. As soon as the prayer time ended, I dashed out of the sanctuary to retrieve Jessica from her classroom.

As I peeked through the doorway to beckon her, someone grabbed my shoulders from behind, twirled me around, and gave me a big hug. It was the young pastor, Keith Butler. "Thank you so much!" he said. "Our church has been going through some severe trials we haven't understood, and we needed to hear that. I love you!"

Riding back to Eureka Springs, Rosie said to me quietly in the back seat, "That was a message from the Lord, because you had no way of knowing what our church has been going through."

I still don't know. But I'm glad I was obedient.

Cuernavaca is called "The City of Eternal Springtime." It lies about 45 miles southwest of Mexico City toward the Pacific coast, and its lower altitude of 5,000 feet lends a warmer climate than Mexico's capital city, which is 7,250 feet above sea level. Dick was glad to move out of the world's biggest metropolis, although he caught a bus back in several days a week, helping the bookstore get back on its feet after moving back into its locale, which had finally been restored after the earthquake.

Dick enjoyed the heat of Cuernavaca, being as he was from the deep south, but I poured perspiration for a whole year till my body adjusted. I renamed it the "City of Eternal Summertime!"

We had looked for a regular church to attend and be active in some area of service. We knew Armando Alducin from Mexico City and heard he had moved to Cuernavaca and started a church in La Selva district. We began attending when we were not out of town and appreciated his excellent preaching and teaching.

We didn't find a place of involvement, however. When we met with him and his wife for breakfast to talk it over, he said, "I don't do door-to-door. That's for the Jehovah's Witnesses. My method is evangelistic breakfasts for businessmen." He also held Bible studies at elite country clubs and concentrated on reaching high society all the way up to the president. We knew we had been dismissed.

"That's good," Dick said to me on the way home. "Someone has to reach the upper class. As for me, I'm going out door-to-door in our area and reach the neighbors because there's no church in our section of town." That's what he did, and that's how our church got started. He invited some neighbors to come in and study the Bible. There were five of us that Sunday evening, July 29, 1989, on Dick's fifty-seventh birthday. One of them was Miriam, age eighteen, who taught catechism in the Catholic Church but was disillusioned because the services were used for political purposes. She was the first to come to Jesus, and she was baptized along with Mauricio, one of the young men, and Gabriela the wife of Benjamin, who had already been baptized in his church in Cuajimalpa.

Progress was slow that first year, however, and Dick felt like giving up when his birthday rolled around again in 1990. "There just isn't enough response," he said.

But reading his Bible one morning, God spoke to him through the story of the fig tree the gardener wanted to cut down (Luke 13:6-9). The gardener was told, "Give it another year. Dig around it, fertilize it, and if it still doesn't produce, then cut it down." Dick decided to give it another year, and during that second year we began to see fruit.

"There's somebody I'd like you to meet," Dick said, after he'd been door-to-door one morning in La Joya area on the highway east of Cuernavaca. "I saw this large house was for sale, so I knocked on the gate. This young housewife answered the door and showed me around the grounds. As we walked around the pool, I felt prompted by the Holy Spirit to tell her my testimony. I don't usually do that, but I told her about the storm at sea and how I had later given my life to Christ."

Whenever Dick met a woman who showed interest, he would bring me her name and address for follow-up. This day he took me to meet Margarita. She and I talked as we did a tour of the house and grounds. As we circled the swimming pool, she said to me, "You have such a deep peace. I want that." Dick offered that if she desired we could meet with her and her husband to study the Bible together. She liked that, and we gave her our address and phone number.

A few months went by, and we had no further contact. Then one day as Dick was walking back from the post office, he passed in front of the Seguro Social hospital. A woman standing there on the sidewalk stopped him. "Don't you remember me?" she asked. "You talked to me and told me your testimony." Of course he remembered. It was Margarita. She looked distraught and began to tell him why.

"Our three-year-old son, Cheo, has had a terrible accident," she said. "We were speeding along the highway going to my village in Taxco when he opened the back door of the car and was thrown out onto the rocks. His head was cut open, and he is in the hospital here."

Cheo began his recovery, and they began coming with their three young sons to the Sunday morning meetings at our house, and we started going to their home once a week to study with them. She and her husband, Elias, both invited Christ into their hearts and began to grow in their faith. "You know what my husband likes about you?" Margarita said to me one day. "When we first came to your house, you came out to the car to greet us barefooted." Apparently that had touched him because in Mexico only the poor in the villages ever go barefooted.

Elias and Margarita had begun to share their newfound joy with all their neighbors and wanted to invite everyone to come join our evening study. Dick wanted to get them grounded first though. On September 1, 1991, after finishing the studies we gave to new believers, they were both baptized there in their pool. It was Margarita's birthday. At the end of September, Dick said they could start inviting their neighbors. They faced many trials, as new believers often do. Elias took Cheo with him on an evangelistic outreach to Monterrey during Holy Week with a group from our fledgling church. When he returned his business began to go under, throwing them into a financial bind. Then their third son, one-year-old Mili, was bitten by a scorpion and was dying. Margarita dashed with him to the neighborhood doctor.

"There's nothing I can do for him," the doctor said. "He's already dying."

"That's why I brought him to you!" Margarita cried out. "He's dying, and there *is* something you can do, and you're going to do it!" He applied a needed antidote, and Mili lived.

Margarita became a soul winner and a prayer warrior, but she had many struggles. When I met her, she had been attending *Neuroticos Anonimos*, and even now when struggles overcame her and she couldn't win victory, we would hear her say, "I'm going back to Neurotics Anonymous! They helped me more than the church is helping me." But because she had learned to pray and take everything to God, she would end up on her knees in persevering prayer and find the help she needed.

She gave birth to a fourth little son who died. She and Elias carried the tiny body into the mountains and buried him there alone.

One of her neighbors, Juanita, who sold chickens on the next street, started coming to study with Margarita. She surrendered her life to Christ, and Margarita began to disciple her. Juanita's little three-year-old daughter, Zaira had leukemia, and the group prayed often for her.

Two other three-year-old children in the area also had leukemia. One was the son of Dr. Miranda, a relative of Elias. He came at times with his wife to our meetings but was resistant, not understanding why God allowed his child to suffer like this. One day Dick asked him, "If God were to heal your son, would you give your life to Him?"

"No," he said. Later the child died.

The other one who had leukemia died also, but little Zaira hung in there precariously. Juanita, though, began to be pressured by the nuns to go back to her religion, scaring her with predictions that if she didn't, her child also was going to die. One day I went with Margarita to see her. We stood by her kitchen table while she said, "I'm leaving your church." I felt my heart drop into my feet, and my whole semblance must have changed because Margarita later commented how stricken I looked.

When you have great joy watching someone come through for the Lord and then see that person turn back, it is almost unbearable. She was firmly decided, however, and unwilling to listen, being no longer able to withstand the pressure. She ignored us after that. I think of Jesus when the rich young ruler turned his back and walked away sorrowful because he had great riches. He could not follow through with Jesus' request. Scripture says that Jesus, beholding him, loved him. I wonder if a tear didn't slip out of His eye as He watched the young man's back fade into the landscape.

Now, many years later, Juanita called and said she wanted to talk to me, so I drove out before the couples' meeting. I sat down in her living room and listened to her. I just let her talk—everything she wanted to pour out. She told about her son's wild lifestyle, her husband's illegal status in the U. S., and her own multitude of illnesses. Nine hard years had gone by since I had seen her.

"I've had one hard thing after another," she said, "beginning with Zaira's sickness. Shall I tell you about that?"

"Yes, tell me," I said. "Tell me about Zaira." This is what Juanita told me.

One night when Zaira was at her worst, she came to sleep in my bed, saying she didn't want to sleep by herself. During that night, I had a dream. I had a jug of oil, and it fell and was spilling out onto the floor. *What is that oil? I don't know about that oil,* I said. *Why is it spilt?* I awoke to find Zaira covered with blood. Her nose had started bleeding, and I couldn't get it stopped. I rushed her to the Social Security Hospital, but the doctor was new and didn't know what to do. He bandaged her nose, which made her swallow the blood, which made her sick, and she suddenly threw up in great torrents all over the nurse. They tried to give her blood but couldn't find her veins, and she was becoming very pale from blood loss.

"This can't go on," I told them. "Send us to Mexico City."

"We can't do that," the doctor said.

"You can't *not* do it!' I told him. "There is no other way. We are going to lose her if this keeps on."

"The City of Eternal Springtime"

They finally got her connected to an intravenous and sent us off with a driver to the D. F. On the way, at the Periferico, Zaira's heart stopped.

"Her heart has stopped beating!" I shouted to the driver. "What are we going to do?"

The driver turned and looked and said, "Turn her intravenous up higher, and put your hands over her heart and pump." Having said that, he turned his siren on full blast and put his foot to the floorboard. I did what he said, and soon got Zaira's heart beating again.

Zaira spoke to me in a soft, faint voice: "Mama, I was leaving. I saw up ahead where I was going, and I was leaving you."

By the time we got to the hospital, her heart had stopped again. I jerked my daughter up with the intravenous still plugged in, and told the driver to let me out at the emergency entrance. The guard standing on duty said no, that we had to go through the paperwork for admission first, but I jumped out and pushed by him and rushed in calling for the doctor in emergency to help. They got her heart started up again, but they couldn't get the tube into her to give her a blood transfusion.

"There's no hope," the doctor said. "There's nothing we can do."

I went into an adjacent room and began to pray. "Dear God," I said, "if this is the time for You to take her, then I give her to You. If You want her to stay on, then You will have to heal her, because her body cannot stand any more of the chemotherapy treatments."

As I finished my prayer, the doctor was calling for me. *She has died*, I thought. *God has chosen to take her home.*

The doctor said, "Good news! We finally got the blood transfusion to work!"

Zaira got well after that and didn't need any more chemotherapy. This month Zaira has her twelfth birthday. She got leukemia when she was three years old. Now she is well. It is a miracle."

"Yes, it is a miracle," I said, amazed, repeating her words. Is the greatest miracle, though, in their hearts? Juanita is back with Jesus. Dr. Miranda and his wife, who lost their little son to leukemia, have expressed that they want to attend church as well.

* * *

We had been renting for thirty years when Dick said, "I think it's time for us to buy a house and stop pouring money into rent." By then OM had become more open to buying property, and George and Drena had bought a house near London. Dick began to check newspaper listings, and we started looking at different possibilities. "There are lots of places in CIVAC," he said.

"I wouldn't like that," I said. "It is right by all the factories. Think of the pollution. What do the initials stand for?"

"*Ciudad Industrial Valle de Cuernavaca*," he said.

"That's it! Industry, smoke, air pollution, soot—" I couldn't stand the thought.

"I've seen it," he said. "It doesn't seem that bad. At least we can take a look at it."

I gave in. We went with the Sweet Home Realtors to see what was available. The houses were built together, much like row houses, and very small. The streets were narrow, many of cobblestone, with minimal traffic. The thing that attracted me, interestingly enough, was the closeness to the neighbors, because we wanted to win them for Christ.

I told my friend Lisa Renz that we were looking at houses in CIVAC and expressed my reservations. "It's a good place to be," she said. "Wind blows over you from the north, and it carries any pollution from your factories down here to us." She laughed at the joke on herself. She and her husband were squatters on communal land south of Cuernavaca and had built their own home in a poor area to begin a church there.

We bought a small, two-story house on *8 Este* between the streets *12 and 14 Norte*.

True to form, Dick started going door to door, introducing himself to our new neighbors and making contacts. Right away he came in excited to announce, "I visited this school up the street that gives classes in English. The teachers are very friendly and interested, and one of them lives around the corner and wants to meet you!"

I went to meet Rita. She was seventy-five years old. I invited her to go to church with us, and she gladly accepted. She told me how she had confessed all her sin to the Lord and even made lengthy lists in order to be sure she did not leave out a single thing. I saw a true heart seeking God.

A few Sundays later, as we stopped the car to let her out at the corner after church, she said, "I'm mad at you."

"Why?" I asked her, surprised.

"Because this morning in Sunday school you asked those two new girls who came if they would like to invite Jesus into their hearts," she said.

"And?" I prompted, standing there on the cobblestone facing her.

"I have been coming with you now for three weeks, and you have never asked me if I would like to invite Jesus into my heart."

"Let's do it," I said. "Can you come over this afternoon?"

She came. She opened her heart to Christ and gave herself totally, unreservedly, to Him.

"I have been searching for Him all my life," she said. "I was born a Catholic, but I was never happy in the Catholic Church. I have studied with the Mormons and the Jehovah's Witnesses and other groups. Now I have found Him. I only wish I could have known Him and told others about Him all my life."

Her only lament was that she had not loved Him from childhood and lived all her years for Him. "I am praying for my whole family to come to know Jesus," she said.

She loved children and later began teaching the young ones in Sunday school—a challenge for anyone. "I'm always asking the Lord to give me 'tips' for teaching the children," she said, "and He does!"

One five-year-old in her class was especially disruptive, and no one wanted him in his or her group. He wasn't learning, and he distracted all the others so they couldn't learn. But word got back to me one day that she had a solution to his terrorizing the class. As soon as he walked in, she pointed her finger at him and said, "You're punished," and he sat very still the whole time. Her "tip" was to "quarantine" him immediately, before damage was done. He sat still and listened, and so did the class.

Rita was born August 19, 1919. On that day in 1999 we celebrated her birthday at the church—this vibrant eighty-year-old teacher who had taught school since she was seventeen.

The following year, still teaching at the English language school, she said excitedly, "I'm going to Zacatecas by bus with our director and other teachers from the school. It's a teacher's convention. I want always to be learning new things to help me in my teaching."

On the overnight trip back from Zacatecas, the bus driver fell asleep near the city of Leon. Some of the passengers were killed. Some were crippled. I went to see Rita at the hospital in Cuernavaca. Her smile lit up the room. "You are the first person to come and see me!" She told me about the accident, how luggage got scattered and personal items lost, but with her same grateful spirit, she gave thanks to God.

The next day I was called into Mexico City for the funeral of Joyce Hemmer, one of the ladies in my

Lomas Bible study. When I got home that evening, Rita had already passed into the presence of Jesus. *I know it was a glorious entry!*

In January of 1993, Nora Sirrs, one of the ladies from the Lomas group, phoned from Mexico City to say her doctors wanted her to go into the American-British Hospital for surgery. We had recently moved into the house we bought in CIVAC, and it was a busy week, and I didn't feel able right then to go into Mexico City; but I got a promise from the ladies that they would call me the moment Nora was able to have visitors, because I wanted to go in to be with her.

When the ladies called that Thursday, it was to tell me Nora had come through the surgery but was in intensive care and could not receive visitors yet. For two days I watched the phone over by the front door as I did my work, listening for the ring to tell me Nora was out of intensive care and I could go visit her. Instead I got the news she had died.

"But, Lord, I wanted to see her," swelled up from the depths of my being.

That night I had a dream.

In my dream, I was traveling through the air on a round, flat flying machine with a ceiling. Suddenly Nora came walking toward me, and I noticed how radiant and young and vibrantly healthy she was. I held out my arms and gave her a big hug. "You look wonderful!" I said. "They did the surgery on Thursday, right?"

"Yes, they did," she replied, smiling at me.

"But they told me—" I started to say, "But they told me you died," but I stopped in mid sentence. How was I going to say that? She was more alive than ever!

I didn't expect the dream. The spontaneous cry that welled up was just a sincere desire to see my friend again. I had not once thought she was going to die. But it was wonderful to have seen her so glorious, and I treasured the dream in my heart.

I went to Christ Church in Mexico City for the funeral, arriving a bit early. The only ones there already were a forlorn, stricken husband and teenage son. I went up to John Sirrs and introduced myself. Words of anguish and anger poured out of him. The doctors had made a mistake, he said. They should never have done surgery where there was scar tissue from radiation treatments. Hopelessness overwhelmed him. Why? he wanted to know. Life had no meaning. This was the end. Nora had ceased to exist.

That's when I knew why I had been given the dream. I was to tell it to him and his son. Nora had not ceased to exist. She was a believer in the Lord Jesus Christ, and she was more alive than ever.

His weary eyes came alive as he listened, and a spark of hope shone through. Others began to arrive at that point and form a line to pay their condolences. So that's all I was able to say, but I'm glad I got to say it. *Thank You, Lord. We sorrow not as those who have no hope.*

On December 20, 1994, the same day the peso devalued, plunging Mexico into a ten-year recession, my beautiful niece Stephanie died. She was the twenty-eight-year-old daughter of my sister Joyce and her husband Bill.

It had been a difficult year all around for us. In fact, we even wondered if we would need to leave Mexico because our support was so low. I lost my appetite in October, and there was nothing I wanted to eat, so it didn't matter that we hadn't much money. Dick's book sales dropped off, and customers who owed him could not pay, so he ended up canceling all their debts.

The volcano Popocatepetl, sixty miles from us, had been threatening to erupt. Cuernavaca was named one of the cities of refuge for any inhabitants of "The Smoking Mountain." I had been watching it from the upstairs hall window of our house in CIVAC ever since we moved there. The schools let all the children out early for Christmas in order to house the refugees that were flooding in.

The day it erupted I was out walking with my neighbor Martita. As we headed back toward our neighborhood, I saw the billowing smoke rising high in the air and said, "Look! The volcano is erupting!"

"No, that's just clouds," Martita said.

But I knew it was the volcano. I'd been watching its smoke ever day and could see the difference. That night Dick and I watched the fiery red spectacle of the exploding mountain close up on our television screen, glad that the thousands who lived on or near its base had all been evacuated.

"The City of Eternal Springtime"

The New Year 1995 dawned with another type of violent eruption—fighting in Chiapas near Mexico's southern border, led by Sub-comandante Marcos.

I continued to be sick all that year with continual weight loss, and the doctors I saw in Mexico could not diagnose the cause. One said gastritis, and one said colitis and told me what *not* to eat. That was no problem, for there was nothing I wanted to eat anyway.

When we visited the Grasmans in Valle de Bravo that fall, Kathy said sadly, "The part of Helen I love is gone."

Dick and I flew to the States on November 13. In Arkansas one of my uncles said, "Where did you leave the rest of you?"

Driving through eastern Arkansas, we stopped to see George and Linda Knoll. As we entered the house, Linda said, "Helen, you are only a shadow of your former self."

We had Thanksgiving with the Griffin clan in Mississippi, and my sister-in-law Betty Griffin handed me a check for $200. "You are not well," she said." When you get to Tulsa, I want you see a doctor."

Linda got me an appointment with the doctor she worked with, Dr. T. L. Carey, originally from South Africa. He listened as I related my symptoms and then said, "I think you have tropical sprue. We can't be certain till we run tests, but it sounds like it."

"How do you spell it?" I asked. "S-p-r-e-w? S-p-r-u-e?" I had never heard the word.

Tropical sprue is what it turned out to be. Dick went ahead back to Mexico as scheduled on December 7, but I got my air ticket extended in order to have medical treatment.

I got to spend Christmas in Booneville with my parents, my two sisters, and other family. It puzzled me that Daddy never once called me by name while I was there. I later wondered if maybe he hadn't recognized me because I was such a skeleton.

My dad was also experiencing some temporary changes. I wrote this little piece about him that year.

The Coal Miner

He's seventy-seven, and his silver hair is peppered with black. It matches the shiny aluminum dinner pail he used to carry into the coal mines each day and carry out again with black coal dust in its crevices.

His lungs are black, too, the doctors say—blacker than they were twenty-two years ago when he retired from the mines. His wife worries. "He stays up coughing at nights," she says, "and I think he's going to cough up his guts."

She sometimes would cling to him when he kissed her goodbye of a morning. Those turned out to be times when fellow miners had given their lives down under the ground. But he always came home, day after day, flinging his round dinner pail on the counter and sitting down with his family around him to wolf down his steaming hot meal—usually fried potatoes and pinto beans.

"The City of Eternal Springtime"

His lanky frame and jagged profile won him the part of Abe Lincoln in the town's 1954 centennial celebration. The black stovepipe hat sat well above his large ears, and he wore the black suit and string bow tie with dignity and reserve.

His sharp mathematical mind calculated columns of figures like an adding machine, and he was a walking history book of his own lifetime, remembering names, dates, and events with precision. His keen instinct for direction could lead you to the exact spot, even when all visible landmarks had disappeared.

His sinewy hands worked at carpentry in his off hours. He would buy an old house, remodel it, and resell at a profit. In his basement workshop, he planed and leveled his wood to perfection. Hard work was his favorite pastime.

But he began losing first what he valued most. He now has blocks of time—say 1976—when he can't remember what happened ... along with yesterday. "And I don't know what day this is," he laments. "I have to keep coming in here to look at the newspaper to see what day it is."

He drives up to Fort Smith, but he becomes disoriented and can't find his way home. That troubles him. He now adds his bank statement many times over and still gets the wrong total. "Would you please check this column of figures for me?" he asks. His deep brown eyes behind the meticulously shined gold-rimmed bifocals are puzzled.

His muscled miner's physique has dwindled to 123 pounds. "All the things I would have loved to eat if I had only been able to buy them," he reminisces. "Now I can have anything I want, and I don't want anything."

Argumentative he used to be when he drank, and irrational, insisting on picayune details and controlling others with a glare.

That, too, is gone. In its place is a gentleness, a tranquility, a tender caring and thoughtfulness—and kind words.

I like these last changes in my dad.

* * *

In 1996 Mark, Joy and the twins came down to Cuernavaca on December 30 for ten days. Austin liked to play with the tiny pieces of the manger scene. I was amazed at his dexterity to be able to put them in their places. I did stencils of the twins on the back patio wall. They took back the video I made of their time here, and it became Willa and Austin's all-time favorite movie to watch, Joy said.

Steve and Stella, Laura, Andrew, and baby Sarah came down to Cuernavaca for Christmas in 1997. "Grandmother's Christmas tree is *alive!*" Laura said. I had bought a little tree in Oaxtepec and planted it in a clay pot. Dick was very sick. We didn't realize how sick he was until after they left.

Here's the story I wrote:

The rain soaked my shoes and coattails as I hunched under the tiny blue umbrella and rang the doctor's doorbell. No one answered. Who would want to be roused at 3:30 a.m. in this downpour? The bell's not working, I concluded, and grabbed a rock near my feet to pound on the metal gate. That activated the cocker spaniel, and immediately an upstairs light flashed on, revealing the doctor's robed figure in the window.

"I need help!" I called out. "My husband can't breathe. Can you come?"

Just a few minutes earlier, Dick had awakened me, gasping and with severe pain in his left rib cage. "Get help quick! Maybe the doctor on the corner could come and give me an injection so I can breathe."

The doctor was only two doors away and came immediately. He checked Dick's throat. "Bronchitis," he said, and he gave him an injection of penicillin. "He'll need five of these injections, twelve hours apart."

He also gave me drops to put in boiling water for him to inhale to open up his bronchial tube. "Keep him closed up in the room. No going out at all."

"I've got to be well for when the kids get here for Christmas," Dick said to me later with his usual determination and goal setting. That gave him only three days! After the fifth injection, he had a nightmare: the penicillin was attacking him instead of battling the infection. "No more penicillin for me!" he declared. His scalp was sunburn red, and his feet swollen to half again their size.

On Christmas morning he surprised the grandchildren with his specialty—hot cakes. They had got used to his being up in the den and not able to play with them as he usually did.

On December 30 he asked our son Steve to drive him to another doctor. He'd almost strangled on his phlegm the night before, not drawing enough air to cough it up.

"Yes, it's bronchitis," the doctor said, looking into his throat. "Take this antibiotic for five days, and don't go out at all."

"Could you please order an X-ray of his lungs?" I asked, suspicious that it was more than just bronchitis. He did, and we zoomed downtown. The technician could have read it for us there, but it would have meant an hour wait, so we opted to take it back to the doctor who had written the order. Parking at the shopping center across from the doctor's, Steve dashed across the highway while I went inside to buy the medicines. Dick, quite weary from the outing, waited in the car.

"The doctor glanced at the X-ray and says it's OK," Steve announced. "It's bronchitis, like he said."

When the new five-day round of antibiotics was up, Dick burst out of the doctor-imposed restraints and back into his work. After bidding Steve and his family goodbye the morning of day five, he turned and began cutting the ream of bananas growing in the front yard. The next morning he was back preaching at church. When I protested, he said, "The doctor said five days!"

Monday morning he rescheduled the 6:00 a.m. prayer meeting for men to 7:00 a.m., but he made no other concessions for himself. At 5:00 Tuesday morning one of the men called to say that his wife's baby was on the way, so it was off to the hospital—a boy!

The next two weeks were a steady stream of visitors, village outreach, discipleship sessions, two Pastors' Alliance meetings, a special missionary speaker, plus the ongoing construction of the church building, getting ready to put the roof on.

Dick was not better. In many ways he was worse. The dry, hacking cough of mid-December now came from deep within his chest, bringing up unsightly matter. He had preached the day before with a glass of water in his hand, taking a sip every few sentences. After the service Thania, one of the young women who teaches at the university and had just returned from break, came up to me and said, "Tell your husband I can get a lung specialist for him if he wants."

"You had better tell him yourself," I said. "Maybe he'll listen to you."

"Lord, I commit him into your hands," was my prayer the next morning as he left in a drizzly rain headed for the men's prayer meeting—exactly one month since I had stood in a downpour trying to awaken the doctor on the corner.

But early the following morning, he said, "Maybe we'd better call Thania and have her get that specialist."

By 12:30 that afternoon, we were at the modern, beautiful *Hospital Cuernavaca,* sitting in the office of Dr. José Ramírez Gama, renowned surgeon and professor in the field of respiratory illnesses. He studied my husband intently. He asked him questions and took his medical history. He listened to his lungs, and he looked at the sputum he coughed up. "This is not good at all," he said. He tested his breathing ability and the amount of oxygen in his blood, gave him oxygen and tested it again.

He took his temperature. "You are an amazing person," he said. "If I had the fever you have, I would be—" He flung his arms wide and threw his white head back, faking delirium. "You have great discipline and self-control."

He looked at the X-ray taken three weeks earlier. His hand swept along the bottom curve of the left lung. "Here is the pneumonia," he said, and indicated the white path it took and how it was really a dark mass that had invaded the whole bottom part of the left lung.

He sent us down a hallway to have another X-ray done, and he slapped it up beside the first one. My mouth fell open. The dreaded white was now covering a great area in the top of the lung as well.

"What's happened?" I asked him. "Has the pneumonia spread all the way up there?"

He shook his head, peering closely at the illumined image. "No, this is not the pneumonia. This is something else—a very dense, dark mass," he said. "I don't know what it is. It could be a tumor. First we've got to treat the pneumonia, then we'll find out."

He sent us home with a prescription for "gigantic doses" of the antibiotic Rocephin by injection. We found out our neighbor Marta next door, between us and the pharmacy, was a nurse. Perfect. The doctor commissioned me to monitor closely Dick's temperature and the aspect of his phlegm and report back daily to him. "It's absolutely necessary that we keep his fever down," he said. So we loaded in the Tylenol.

Dick had not been able to lie down to sleep because of the cough and the pain in his side. He slept either partially sitting up in the recliner or propped up in bed with a mountain of pillows.

That night we were sleeping side by side in our king-size bed. I didn't realize it then, but perhaps because of the oxygen and breathing treatment that day plus the doses of Tylenol, he was able to sleep. I was accustomed to listening to his cough and labored breathing throughout the night.

I suddenly awakened at midnight. The clock on the nightstand glowed 12:12 in red numerals. Why was everything so quiet? Where was Dick? Had he gone to the den or maybe downstairs? He sometimes did, thinking it would help me to sleep better. I reached over expecting to feel the empty bed, and my hand touched his bare elbow. It felt hard and cold, and alarm shot through me. I sprang from the bed and dashed to the bathroom in panic. I used the bathroom quickly and slowly washed my hands. You've got to go back in there, I told myself, and see if he is all right. I had never been more scared in my life.

I crept back into the darkened room and bent over where his head lay on the pillow. "Honey, are you all right?" I whispered.

"Yes," came the low murmur. I crawled back in on my side of the bed, elated and grateful, and listened as the pounding of my heart gradually abated.

"Why did you wake me to ask me if I was all right?" he queried the next day.

"I couldn't hear you breathing, and it scared me."

The next night our son Mark in Oklahoma had a nightmare that his father had died and sent us an e-mail about it.

It was a long week. Hordes of visitors came. Everybody brought fruit. Dick, who normally loves fruit and eats several pieces a day if it's around, was repulsed by the thought of it.

I began to receive people in the lawn chairs out front, so it wouldn't be so tiring for him, and let one person go in to have a prayer with him.

That week for the first time I felt alone. I knew the Lord was with me, and I told Him so, and the days saw no lack of people around; but the weight of the responsibility of my husband's life, which seemed to be in peril, was on me alone. Shouldn't he be in the hospital? It seemed we were at the ends of the earth, and the nights were especially dark.

Dick missed church that Sunday for the first time. But he had been feverish during the night, not getting to sleep till 3:00 a.m. and up again at 7:00 a.m. He answered when my mother phoned and asked her to have the church there in Arkansas pray for his tests the next day.

Later he conceded, "I could never have made it to church today."

We arrived early Monday morning at the Hospital Cuernavaca to see the doctor and have a CAT scan done. He read in detail the reports he had asked me to bring in of Dick's surgery in 1974, when he'd had his right eye removed because of a malignant tumor. The doctor thought a cancer cell had remained in his body all this time and suddenly, aggressively showed up in his lung.

I sat outside the radiation department for the hour it took to do the CAT scan. Dick had wanted me to go in with him, but the radiologist said there was no reason to expose me to unnecessary risk. The radiologist finally came out, looking like the mad scientist, his hair askew and his arms flailing. It's not good, I thought. Then the doctor came sailing by and told us to go directly for another X-ray.

Back in the doctor's waiting area, he said, "We've got to do surgery within seventy-two hours. Go on home, and I'll contact you after we've got the complete reading from the CAT scan."

An emaciated woman, sitting there and overhearing, said to me, "He's an excellent surgeon. He operated on my lung a year ago." I thought to myself, *Lady, you're not a showroom specimen for the benefits of lung surgery. Let me out of here.*

Dick and I talked when we got back to the house. "I feel the need of family," I said. "We're so far away from everyone down here." He agreed. "You're probably going to have a lengthy recuperation time," I added, "and I don't like the idea of being here all alone, just the two of us."

As we discussed flying up to the States for treatment, we both felt an engulfing peace. We called his brother Buddy in Florida. "I'm behind you whatever you decide to do," he said.

Dick wanted to wait two days, though, to have a meeting with the church leaders and give everyone instructions.

"No!" Buddy said. "Your health is more important. You are to fly up first thing in the morning."

R-r-r-r-ing. It was the specialist. "I've just come from a consultation with a number of my colleagues," he said. "We are almost sure it's not cancer but a very large lung abscess. I have made all arrangements for your husband to be admitted at 8:30 in the morning for immediate attention."

I told him of our decision to fly to the States where we would be near family. "That decision is yours," he said. "I won't pressure you, but I do recommend you stay and check in as I have said because of the urgency of this case." We knew he was concerned for us, but the peaceful waters of my soul became agitated. "If you change your mind," he said, "just show up. Your admission is all arranged." Click.

Later Thania also called, with the same insistence, and I felt the same turmoil. But when we reaffirmed together our decision to fly to the States for treatment, the peace returned.

I felt as though we fled, like the children of Israel with the Egyptian chariots in pursuit. Buddy's son, Tommy, a medical doctor, had warned us of the risk of flying at high altitude with a severely abscessed lung. It could burst, and the lung could collapse. So it was with immense relief that we touched down in Tulsa all intact.

Dr. Carey fit us in that same evening after his other appointments. He grabbed a phlegm specimen as soon as Dick coughed and labeled it for the lab. "We need to know the strain of bacteria," he said, "in order to give the specific antibiotic." Meanwhile he started him on amoxicillin, which works with several types, and ordered more X-rays. In the suddenness of leaving, we had been denied access to the X-rays and CAT scan locked up in the *Hospital Cuernavaca*. Thania rushed them up later by courier.

Between that night and the next morning, a wonderful thing occurred: all three of our sons arrived with their families. Mark, Steve, and Philip accompanied us to see the doctor. The three of them were sitting side by side in Dr. Carey's waiting room when Linda burst in from her office next door, waving a fax. "The results of the CAT scan arrived from Mexico," she sang, but then her face fell. "It's all Spanish!"

No problem, we all thought as we looked at each other. Mark and Steve both teach Spanish at Oklahoma City University, and Philip, a pastor in Beaumont, Texas, teaches Spanish part-time in a local Christian high school. Mark rose, took the fax, and went with Linda to her office to do the official translation.

That day, having verified the strain of bacteria in his lung as streptococcus, Dr. Carey started Dick on seven days of intravenous antibiotics, the same kind the specialist in Cuernavaca had been giving by injection. My sister Linda, then director of Dr. Carey's home health agency and an experienced nurse, took quality care of him there in her home. We even had a special living area she and her husband had added on to their house the year before for a client of hers. A load was lifted from me that I had been more than willing to carry but under which I felt incapable: intensive health care.

Having our sons and their families there for two days infused new strength. We had left our kin and our homeland at the beginning of the 1960s to serve the Lord in Mexico and did not flinch. Our sons, who had been born and raised in Mexico, had now married and been living in the States and Canada. But they needed us at this time, just as we needed them.

After seven days of superior care in the Wilands' home, Dick entered the hospital for seven days to have his lung drained. Mark came back to help me check his dad in that Wednesday morning. Dr. White, in charge of the procedure, extracted an initial 110 cubic centimeters of abscess.

Friday morning Pastor Jim King from Booneville, Arkansas, drove 150 miles with his wife Judy, my sister Joyce, and Joe Parnell to visit Dick. They joined the doctors that morning in earnest prayer for his healing.

That night Dr. Prost came in and injected two large vials of streptokinase into Dick's lung to help dissolve the stubborn remaining abscess so it would flow out. "If it doesn't," he said, "we will have to do surgery. No abscess can remain in the lung, and there's no other way to get it out."

The injection worked! So on Monday the main hose that had been pumping for six days got whisked away, and on Tuesday we bade a glad farewell to St. John Medical Center, reassuring the staff that we had home health care set up. Linda continued the intravenous antibiotics until Friday, and Dick finally got free of the needle in his arm after seventeen days. She suctioned more cc's daily for still another week through the small blue tube that dangled from his back. On its seventeenth day, Dr. Carey pulled it out.

During that last week, Dick's brother Billy and his wife Betty drove all the way from Greenville, Mississippi, and we celebrated Billy's birthday together. What a blessing family is! We had missed out on being with family for over thirty-seven years, except for occasional visits, forsaking all to follow Christ and serve on the mission field.

I had thought often about His promise to give us "a hundred times more in this present life, with persecutions." We had experienced family a hundred times over in Mexico—fathers, mothers, sisters, brothers, sons, daughters, even grandchildren—and persecutions as well. I thought the promise had been fulfilled in this lifetime.

But He poured it on, a hundred times more, and in a way I had never expected, in giving me back those I had originally forsaken to follow Him. In the second month of recuperation, we had the great pleasure of visiting with each of our sons again, this time in their own homes. We were able to be together with my two brothers and two sisters and each of their spouses to celebrate our parents' sixtieth wedding anniversary. Dick preached again for the first time in two months, and for the first time in my hometown, with an abundance of extended family present. *God isn't anybody's debtor.*

* * *

My father passed away on July 21, 1998. When I called his hospital room earlier, he had trouble hearing. "You'll have to talk to your mother. She'll tell me what you say," he said, and he passed the phone to the wife he had cherished for over sixty years.

That was the last time I talked to him. When I flew up to Houston, my flight was delayed forty-five minutes leaving Mexico City. By the time I got through U. S. customs and dashed to the gate, my connecting flight had departed, the last flight out.

He died that night while I slept in a luxury hotel in downtown Houston, courtesy of the airlines as I awaited a morning flight. I arrived in Booneville in time to help my siblings make funeral arrangements. When the funeral director looked down at his information, he said, "Your father was a Mason. Do you want them to take part in the service?

I shouted, "No!" without even looking at the others to get their opinion. In my mind he left the Lord and the church when he joined the Masons. Only when they forsook him during his bouts with alcoholism did he forsake them.

After the funeral I looked at the beautiful headstone he and Mother chose, had engraved, and put on their plot at the Oak Hills Cemetery in Booneville.

Daddy's side had the Masonic emblem cut into the stone, and it grieved me. Mother's had an open Bible. Then I went around to the back, where Mother had the engravers write the words from the last two verses of Romans 8:

> *For I am persuaded, that neither death, nor life, nor angels, nor principalities, nor powers, nor things present, nor things to come, nor height, nor depth, nor any other creature, shall be able to separate us from the love of God, which is in Christ Jesus our Lord. (Rom. 8:38-39 KJV)*

She had shown it to me some years back and said, "It costs a lot for each letter, so we had the engravers omit every "nor" except the last one. I read it again, beginning with "neither death" and finishing with "nor any other creature shall be able to separate us from the love of God."

I was suddenly comforted, and the emblem on the front of the headstone faded in importance. I remembered Linda had told me that Daddy's last words before he died were, "I love God. I love God." And I remembered Rev. Parker's words to me when I was fifteen years old: "God will bring him back before he dies." *Nothing shall be able to separate us.*

Ada's Noises

Ada's husband died in March six years after we bought the CIVAC house and moved in. Ada came over after that, at our invitation, and we had prayer with her. I'd always spoken to her when I saw her outside, but she had been sick since I got back from Daddy's funeral, and Rita had been to see her and pray with her.

Ada was our neighbor over the back wall. She was aged and hunchbacked from decades as a seamstress.

The night her husband died, I was awake most of the night wondering at all the unearthly noises coming through our bedroom window. I concluded he had died because I heard the wailing, but I didn't know for sure till later. It sounded as though someone was digging for hours in their back patio, which joins ours and is divided only by a slender, red brick wall. In my fertile imagination, they were burying the body there. After that night, their back patio started getting cemented over, a section here, a section there, and I wondered about that too. No more patches with grass or flowers. We invited Ada over one evening to a prayer meeting so we could pray for her. She was very happy to have us do that.

One day she was given a colorful rooster from a client in her home state of Oaxaca. Dick went over to talk to her about the cock-a-doodle-do that was keeping us awake, especially him, crowing at all hours of the night. Could nothing be done? No, she said, there was nothing she could do about it because it was a gift from a client in Oaxaca—end of conversation. I learned to live with the rooster and sleep through it, but Dick suffered significant sleep loss for over two years from what I nicknamed "Jet Lag Rooster," whose body clock ran seriously amok.

Later a granddaughter and her husband came to live with Ada. They put up a small vegetable stand at their front gate just around the corner from us. One morning as I was walking by, I stopped to look at their vegetables. On one corner of the table I saw a double breast of chicken. That's unusual, I thought. They always sell only vegetables. I need some chicken, though. I'll just buy from them. I cooked it way beyond the point of well done, but it was still not tender. I went ahead and served our plates. Dick and I chewed and chewed and chewed on the toughest chicken we have ever eaten. But we laugh about it today, because we never heard the rooster crow again!

Sometime after that, over a back wall I began to be bombarded every midday for two hours with unearthly noises like a child gone wild with an electric guitar. There was no rhyme or reason, just a conglomeration of metallic sounds; there was no tune, no beat, just harsh electronic twanging and screeching like some game-room machine gone mad. I started praying against it, because if it was music, which I could not conceive it to be, it was out of the pit and designed to drive one insane. A few days later, a handsome young fellow came knocking at the gate and introduced himself as Ada's grandson who had moved here from another state. Had we by any chance seen his Siamese cat with the green eyes? he wondered. I told him no, that if any cat came around our little dog Ladybug chased it off, but I would keep a lookout for it. I asked him how he liked living here and whether the noise at noon everyday bothered him. He looked puzzled, so I tried to describe it. "Oh, that's rock music," he said. I don't know if I inadvertently happened to ask the right person, but the horrendous playing stopped after that, saving my sanity. Thank You, God, for huge favors!

Ada died, and another young couple moved in. They also may have been grandchildren. The pretty wife had wavy peroxide blonde hair, and the husband was tall, dark, and serious. The first day they did laundry, I thought, *That washing machine is on its "last leg." It's not going to last more than a week before it breaks down completely.* I couldn't have been more mistaken. It ground out clothes day after day after day, load after load after load for over two years. How could they do so much wash?

Simultaneously, another noise started up that I could not identify. At first I thought it might be a siren call from one of the factories, announcing their change of shifts, but since it didn't stop, it couldn't be that. Besides, it sounded more like a drill. Maybe some neighbor was drilling holes to hang pictures or doing a minor construction job and would soon be through. But no, it kept on day after day, hours on end, permeating the whole house. There was no room where I could get away from it.

Walking around the corner in front of Ada's house, I saw what it was. The serious young husband and his helper were taking the faded paint and rust off two old cars right there in their front yard and in the street in front of their house. Well, maybe when they finished, the unbearable noise would be gone. But when they finished with those two, three more came to take their place, and more after that. I asked my neighbor Marta, my walking partner, if the constant shrill drilling sound did not bother any of the other neighbors. She didn't know, she said, because her teenager puts his music on so loud she couldn't hear anything else anyhow, and his music was driving her crazy.

"The City of Eternal Springtime"

My husband felt there must be some stipulation against setting up a car body shop in a residential area. One day after my walk with Marta and praying very much about what, if anything, to do, I spotted the man right there in the street at the back end of a car "drilling" off the old paint. The noise was so loud he had to turn it off so we could talk.

"You're doing a great job on these cars," I said. "They turn out looking beautiful."

"Yes," he replied, holding his buffer midair. "Whenever your husband wants me to do his car, I will."

"Thanks, I'll tell him," I said, "but isn't this an awful lot of noise for a residential area?"

"That's why I'm out here in the street: so the sound won't bother people inside their houses."

"But it permeates the whole atmosphere," I said. "There's no place in my house where I can get away from it."

He nodded and went back to his work.

Dick was happy when I told him about my chat with the neighbor. "Maybe it'll make a difference," he said. "Did you mention the washing machine too?"

No, I hadn't. One giant at a time, I guess.

Some time went by with no change, so I stopped to chat again.

"How's it going?" He was reluctant to stop his work with just one patch of aqua blue left on this old car. But he shut off the buffer.

"I'm getting a shop downtown," he replied. "It's going to be ready a week from Monday."

"That's wonderful," I said. "Could I ask you one more question?" He lowered his buffer. "The washing machine—" I ventured. "Your wife does so many loads of wash every day."

"Yes, that's because we get our clothes extremely dirty in this kind of work."

"Well, the noise the washer makes, like metal scraping on metal, isn't there some way to fix it?"

"No, there's nothing that can be done," he stated flatly, in dismissal.

Eventually, though, the body shop got moved out. Sometimes he'd still do work there, but it was minimal. What never let up one bit was the laundry service. In fact, it increased to many loads a day with forty-minute long agitation cycles. I dubbed it "the eternal scraping."

I tried ignoring it. But it filled every room of the house except Dick's den and study, and I couldn't do any of my work in there. I tried pretending it was beautiful, like a lullaby, rocking, rocking, rocking, but that was like pretending the alligator is a cute little lizard. I tried putting on music to cover it up, but I had to put it on so loud I didn't enjoy it.

As the months went by, I continually prayed, "Lord, help me to handle this. Why do I have such a hard time with this? What can I do to learn to bear it?" One day I tried ignoring it by making use of the time to pray. I decided that very time the scraping started, I would get down on my knees and pray. When it stopped, I could get up and do my work. But after about two hours praying, it was still going, and I ended up in tears.

I tried praying against it: "If you say to this mountain, be removed and be cast into the sea, believing in your heart it will be done, it will be done." But that didn't work. Maybe I didn't believe enough, or the washing machine didn't qualify as a mountain. It was mountainous to me, though, and I continually asked the Lord what He wanted to show me through this, or what He wanted me to do.

That spring a maintenance crew was sent by my friend, Janis Reed, to do some repair jobs on our house. I asked the man in charge to observe the machine in action from my bedroom window. "Can it be fixed?" I asked. He looked dubious. The whole thing would have to be taken apart to get at the cause of the problem, he said.

A college girl named Laura came down that summer. "Can't you just get over it?' she asked. "Like, what's your problem?"

"I might say that to someone who cringes when fingernails are raked down a blackboard," I said, "because I can handle that particular noise. I could manage to live with the rooster. I could abide crying babies, barking dogs, howling cats, bongo drums beating in the park catty-cornered from us at every full moon, and melancholy drunks across the street warbling off-key. I even managed to live four years above a trucking service that revved up its motors at four in the morning, one block from the constantly zooming traffic of the biggest avenue in Mexico City.

"And I love *real* music," I explained to her, "but for some reason electronic, metallic noises do me in." I could not live with the electronically generated rock or the shrill drill—nor could I live with the eternal scraping. I could escape it if I must by closing all the doors and windows, shutting myself in the den upstairs, and putting music on, but that was temporary and impractical with Cuernavaca's heat. Windows and doors are left open, and ceiling fans are used to survive the heat. I could always leave the house. But why should somebody else's noise drive me out of my own house?

We had lived in Mexico forty years, and our three sons were born and grew up in Mexico. That summer when I was with Philip, who is a pastor in Beaumont, Texas, he asked me, " Mom, are you happy in Mexico?" I told him how I would be except for the "eternal scraping." I felt down on myself for letting a small matter like that affect me. He's pragmatic, and he offered a simple solution: buy them a new washing machine. I'd thought about that. Maybe I should follow through on that.

Before my birthday Dick and I talked about having the back wall built up higher. We'd talked about that at different times since the rooster days and even got Ada's permission at one point to build up her wall since the brick wall that was there was hers. I wanted to build with stone, like the rest of our own wall, but Dick saw the problem of digging down for a foundation since everything was cemented in and we didn't know what pipes, etc. might be underneath.

We went away for my birthday, and I had three glorious days of relaxation away from scenes of the bombed-out site of the *Twin Towers* and

"The City of Eternal Springtime"

around-the-clock rescue work and CNN's continual breaking news on *America's New War*—and my own private war against a washing machine.

On that Friday after returning, I did all my laundry: three washer loads plus a bucket of hand washables. A young girl washed clothes all day long and chitchatted at great length with a neighbor boy through their back fence. So the "eternal scraping" never ended, but it was blocked out a bit by the hum of my own washer and dryer while I had them going, and the computer while I worked, and some music videos I put on. A couple times I noticed their washer was grinding away with none or very few clothes in it. At the end of the day, it started to sprinkle, and I dashed out to bring in the hand wash I'd left drying on the line. For me it was the end of a Friday workday and time for things to quiet down, but suddenly the grating of the washing machine split the evening air. "Oh, Lord," I breathed quietly and let the lid of my washing machine fall shut with a bang.

With the load of dry clothes over my shoulder, I was poised to open the kitchen door when I heard the girl say, "*Si no le gusta el ruido, que regrese a su país*" (If she doesn't like the noise, let her go back to her own country).

I knew she wasn't speaking to me, but in a calm voice, I answered, "*No me gusta el ruido, es cierto—y ya tengo dos años escuchandolo*" (I don't like the noise, that's true—and I've been listening to it for two years now.)

Everything got very quiet. I was in shock as I went back into the house. Who was that girl anyhow, and how did she know I didn't like the noise? She was probably shocked too—first that her voice was audible to me, and second that I spoke Spanish. How eerie that she should say, "Let her go back to her own country," because that is exactly what I had often been driven to contemplate when I thought I couldn't stand it anymore.

After a bit I went upstairs and said to Dick, "I had a conversation with somebody over the wall." I related the brief interchange.

"Is that all?" he asked.

"Yep, that's all," I said. "I just think it would be interesting to ask her if I happened to be a Mexican and didn't like the noise what she would recommend I do."

The next five days were unbelievably quiet. My house had the feel of recuperating to health after some horrible malignancy had been removed. Wow, I thought, this is what normal can be!

The calm didn't last, though. After five days they were back in business, and that was the morning I woke up with a vicious sore throat, so sore I could hardly swallow.

I had it in my heart to go see them, though, and apologize for my impatience. I didn't want to create any unnecessary rift. I had gone over the end of July and given them an invitation to our church's anniversary, and I wanted to be a witness to them. I watched and waited for the opportunity, but my sore throat developed into a terrible cold, and I wasn't seeing many people. So I waited it out.

"The City of Eternal Springtime"

When Dick threw out the garbage on Thursday, he said he saw the man and didn't speak to him, because he was making a front wall, but he greeted him as he came back. "That's good," I said.

Early Friday morning Dick left with a team to Tetela, Oaxaca. I got to have the weekend alone to meditate and pray, read and study, and also relax and get well. There was been no "eternal scraping" the whole time—a marvelously quiet and lovely weekend. I would have gone to church but was still hoarse and stuffy. I called Dick to see how he and the team were doing, and he agreed I should stay back.

In my devotional time and prayer that morning, I noted how my sickness, which had hung on, had coincided with the emotion created for me by the washing machine. I need to resolve this, I thought, and I will be well. I prayed for Him to anoint me with His Spirit to do it.

This was God's timing. I felt total calm as I went to the gate and knocked. The young girl came out. We greeted each other and smiled. I told her I would like to talk to them a minute, but she said the couple wasn't home, that they had just left and would be back in about two hours. I told her that I had come to apologize for my impatience. She looked at me, surprised, but didn't comment. I gave her my phone number so she could let me know when they got back. Then I could come back or they could come over, either way. She smiled, a very pretty and happy girl.

I made a list of things to perhaps say to them: (1) they were nice neighbors, (2) today my husband and I celebrate nine years since moving into this house,

(3) we knew Ada from the time we moved in and knew when her husband died, and (4) I would like to help them to repair or replace the washing machine.

I had gone at 11:30 in the morning. They never called, and I didn't hear them come back, so I waited. I went back over about 5:00 p.m. The car was back, the front door was open, and windows were open, but a padlock was on the front gate, and nobody answered when I knocked two different times. I called out *"Buenas tardes,"* but there was not a sound. Maybe they're having a nap, I thought.

I felt good that I went. The main thing I wanted to say I was able to say, and she must have been the person who needed to hear it.

Sam and Carrie Clark with Navigators came to minister in our church one weekend. Dick left early out to the church to help get things set up, and the three of us lingered at the breakfast table. Suddenly Sam said, "What is that horrendous noise?"

A discordant grating had cracked the still morning air. "It's the neighbor's washing machine," I said and gave them a short history of my struggles in regard to it.

He listened, and then he said, "This is an attack from the enemy who wants you to leave here. We're going to pray against it." He led us in prayer. Then he pulled out a little three-by-five card and began to jot down Scripture references from the Psalms. "These are Scriptures you can use to pray against it," he said, handing me the card as we left for church.

Sometimes we entertain angels unawares.
* * *

"The City of Eternal Springtime"

Chapter 6

The 2000s
The Desires of Our Hearts

I had an e-mail from Mamie Beck, a teacher in Philip's church. I met Mamie when she spoke at the *Christ Community Church* retreat for the ladies in May of 2000. I didn't realize she even knew who I was in the crowd. The following May, 2001, when I did the retreat, she contacted me to say how sorry she was she couldn't attend, but her semi-invalid husband had recently had surgery. She asked if I could give her a couple days later during my trip when we could meet and talk. She would even be willing to come to Arkansas while I was there. Well, it didn't work out that summer, and all of a sudden I heard from her again. She wrote about her situation and then said,

> *Enough about me ... I feel impressed to ask you what you desire. Woman to woman ... is there anything you would like to have that I can send*

> *you? It would be my delight to be able to give you the desires of your heart right now. Remember: ask and you will receive. Don't ask for your needs; ask for the desires of your heart. You have been delighting yourself in the Lord, and He is willing to give you the desires of your heart. ASK!*

I didn't know what to say and waited a whole week before answering. The night I wrote, I mentioned different things I enjoyed and desired, not knowing exactly what she was offering, and tucked in among a number of things, I said,

> *When Dick read your letter, he immediately said, "A trip." He knows how much I have wanted to be "home" in the States this year for Christmas, but for some reason I didn't have peace about pursuing it and have only experienced peace as I laid it on the altar.*

I felt I had presented it in such a way that if she hadn't intended something that big, then she could dismiss it and go for the kind of book I liked to read, or the scrapbooking materials, or encouraging me in the kind of writing I wanted to do. But by the next afternoon, there was an e-ticket on my computer, round-trip all the way to Beaumont.

In my heart I had been longing to know what it was like in the U.S. How were my fellow Americans faring after the 9-11 attacks on our nation. Three months and two days had passed. I wanted to be there and feel what people were feeling.

I found a seat in the crowded Houston airport to await my connecting flight on to Beaumont and began a conversation with the Indian lady sitting next to me wearing the traditional *sari*. "I just flew in from New York City," she said. "I'm waiting for the connecting flight on to Beaumont, where I'm spending Christmas with my daughter who's a medical doctor there."

"You flew in just now from New York City?" I said, amazed.

"Yes," she said. "I worked at the Twin Towers. I was to have been at work that day ..." I listened while she recounted the events and was amazed that God gave me those two hours of layover with that beautiful woman from India and I was able to hear her story and give praise to God with her!

"You're going to Beaumont to see your daughter! I'm on my way to Beaumont to see my son!

Philip put me to work right away teaching and counseling women in the church and also helping Deanna because she'd had major surgery on December 3.

The big Christmas get together in Tulsa was rescheduled for December 23, and even Mark was back from Singapore that day and got to be there with his family. The kids were darling in their Singaporean outfits, and Joy looked elegant with her new hairstyle. The other desire of my heart—to be together, all five of us kids with Mother—was granted. My brother Alton had dialysis that day and was wiped out, but we were all five there with our mother for the party and gift exchange.

Down in Booneville I had Christmas Eve with my mother, and the two of us traveled with Joyce and Bill to Harrison for a big family dinner on Christmas Day with Bill's mother and all ten of her children and their families. Before it got dark, Mother and I drove out with Joyce to put an angel on Stephanie's grave. She had died seven years before, and it was my first time to visit there.

The special family Christmas filled up my deeply felt need to experience the season with extended family. I got to be with Mark and Joy and the kids for New Year's. They had a lot of friends over to celebrate. I made it back to Beaumont in time to do a final workshop in Philip's church before joining Dick again in Cuernavaca on January 8.

The next morning, January 9, 2002, I looked down at the morning paper lying on the desk. Then I looked again and rubbed my left eye. Something was distorting the letters and cutting a little zigzag on the newsprint wherever my left eye focused. What on earth was wrong with my eye?

Rita's granddaughter had studied medicine at the university, and she recommended an excellent eye doctor, a professor of hers. He did several studies and tests, and when I went back he was accompanied by another specialist called in from Mexico City. They explained the problem: a small opening in the macula behind my eye, which would require surgery to correct.

I was shocked. I was jolted at the thought of surgery in the back of my eye. I excused myself a moment and found the ladies room, shut the door, and stood gazing at my startled reflection in the mirror. I wanted to burst into tears.

A thought suddenly came to me, though, as I stared at myself in the glass: *The Lord already knew all about this ahead of time. It's a shock to me, but it was not a surprise to Him at all.*

Peace flooded my being. Not only did He know, but He was also in charge.

I flew up to Beaumont for the surgery, and Philip and his family and church were a wonderful support system during the arduous recovery period, when I had to keep my head down, face parallel with the floor, day and night during the healing process. It was to keep the back of the eye dry so it could heal properly. "Mom, head down!" rang out quite often around the house those two weeks.

People from the church brought meals every day in a marvelous display of hospitality. I was able to spend precious time with Mamie, too, who had paid my way at Christmas, and also be a guest in the home of Sissy, who hosted Mamie's weekly Bible study for women. The surgeon and the Baptist Hospital were most gracious too in giving me a generous missionary discount.

Would the noises over the back wall ever come to an end? I'd been back almost four weeks after having the eye surgery. The first four days were very quiet and wonderful; then the neighbors "mopped up" for three days, especially with the shrill drill. Then there were four days more of silence, and then "mop up" time again with shrill drill and a newborn exercising its lungs nonstop.

Then suddenly all noises stopped, and everything became blissfully quiet for two weeks. Black plastic sacks tied to the front fence blocked any view in except where some had slipped loose. I could see the little white dog peering hungrily through the rails. *"Lord, I have never felt so happy in my house. It seems like my house again. The invaders are gone. The birds are singing their hearts out in the back patio now."*

On July 22, 2002, I happened to look out my bedroom window, and I saw a different clothesline and different clothes hanging out. What? How could clothes be hanging out to dry when I hadn't heard the washing machine? Then I looked down where the eternally scraping square yellow washer used to sit. There in its place sat a cute round one. Incredible! It had done a load of wash, and I hadn't heard a sound! *New neighbors have moved in. "Thank You, Lord, from the bottom of my heart."*

* * *

Our church made a journey down into the southern Sierra Madre mountain range in the state of Guerreo to a village of four thousand of the Yoloxochitl dialect of Mixteco Indians.

The year before Rev. Moises Lopez came as the main speaker for our October missions conference and challenged the church to "adopt a village." When I heard it, I thought, *What? Adopt a village? How do you do that? We don't want to adopt a village.*

It's good I kept the words to myself, because that was precisely what God had in mind for us to do—adopt an ethnic village in one of the remote areas of Mexico to reach it with the gospel.

I stood nearby, watching as each of the church elders signed the adoption certificate for the Mixteco village of Yoloxochitl. You could see the certificate hanging on the wall at the back door of the sanctuary. The church prayed for nine whole months before going for the first time to this remote village in the mountains. The elders went first to "spy out the land."

Dick actually felt some fear about going because of stories he had heard. What if they did more to them than just refuse them entrance? A few days before leaving, though, God gave him a dream. In the dream he saw himself standing in the village with the headman welcoming them. He felt a reassurance and peace of mind about God having prepared the way ahead of them.

He arrived with the elders to a village they thought was Yoloxochitl. As they climbed down out of the van, Dick looked around but thought, *This is not the village I saw in the dream.* Moreover, he did not see the man he had seen in the dream. They began to inquire, and the townspeople said, "You are not there yet. You must go on up the hill."

After a long, difficult drive up the winding dirt road, Dick recognized the streets of the village as soon as they entered. There was the headman, also, just as he had seen in his dream, to welcome them. Later this village chief said to them, "I don't know why we allowed you to come in. We have refused all others who have tried to enter."

Dick and the elders knew why. Months of prayer and seeking God had prepared the way.

I was able to go on a later trip to Yolo. I like traveling and prepared myself for adventure and some hardships as seven of us crammed into the church van packed with Alfonso and Luchita's washing machine and multiple household items and food supplies. It was 3:45 a.m. when I squeezed in with Chayo on my right and a long cardboard box full of bread blocking the window to my left. The corner of the box kept bumping Dick's head as he sat slumped on two cushions atop the spare tire at my feet.

With the two drivers up front, Jose Luis Angeles and Jose Luis Hernandez, we sailed down the luxurious toll road to Chilpancingo. Then we turned onto a lesser and rougher highway almost to the Pacific coast, and then up the dusty, winding mountain road full of crevices into a magnificent panoramic view of mountains all around and river below. We pulled up in front of the brick-and-adobe house of Don Zenón, one of the village patriarchs, at 2:35 p.m., almost eleven hours later. We had followed Alfonso and his family, who had left at midnight to get a head start since their car had been overhauled, and he needed to drive slowly. We caught up with them for lunch at the bottom of the Yolo mountain. I chuckled, watching two geese stick long white necks through their wooden crate in the overloaded overhead carrier to honk at us.

While we were in that little town of San Luis Acatlán, a tired, thin woman named Eudita and her daughter came into the restaurant, where we had bought water and soft drinks. We learned she had lost fourteen family members in the terrible bus crash near Guadalajara about ten days before. They were traveling as part of a pilgrimage with the *Luz del Mundo* sect. As we refreshed ourselves with the cold drinks, Chayo talked to her about the Giver of living water and God's great plan of salvation offered to her. She received Him into her life that day and went on her way joyful.

Alfonso parked his car across the street from Don Zenón's, and we visited with the family and took "showers" with a bowl and bucket of water inside a little brick structure covered with vines next to where the women were scaling fresh fish for supper. The two geese, recently freed from their cages, ran around the bare courtyard with all the turkeys, chickens, pigs, and an occasional dog.

Luchita got restless for the key to the house they'd rented, so she and I walked over to the Comisario to see what we could find out. I got to meet the headman and his wife Aurora and their children. Aurora had their eight-year-old daughter Kenya bring us cold drinks, and we talked.

"Sra. Lucia knows you're here," the headman's wife said, "but she has shut herself in a room upstairs at the school, saying you are not to have the key until she says so." H-m-m. Cool welcome.

It was about 6:00 p.m. when Luchita finally got news that Sra. Lucia would see her. I walked with her to the owner's house and met this woman who wouldn't look me in the eye. Later I learned that she practiced witchcraft.

The house was nice enough, and she had done a lot of work around the outside. We prayed as we scrubbed and swept and the men unloaded the stuff. Luchita had had a bad dream about the house and the great stack of lumber taking up about a quarter of the main room. Her misgivings began to evaporate, though, as we prayed and sensed God moving in the village and wanting to do a work in Sra. Lucia as well. I found a broken candlestick at the back door. I fitted the jagged glass together and read about the "seven spirits of Africa" and their powers invoked though the candle, and I prayed against any lingering influences from it in the house.

When the men finished unloading, Dick settled down on the front step and started singing to a dozen young boys who'd followed him into the yard. I liked the scene and pulled out my little video camera. Up until now I had asked permission before taking a picture, but since we were in Alfonso and Luchita's house and I was going to focus on Dick, I started to turn it on. Immediately, two young boys took flight like startled birds, flailing their arms, and they didn't stop running for about the length of a football field. I put the camera away, and when they reappeared, I apologized for frightening them.

Back at Don Zenon's we feasted on the fresh fried fish with hot handmade tortillas and salsa. Later we sat in a circle and sang and talked. Rafael, his schoolteacher son, said the wood should be moved, and he knew where it could be stored. I was relieved. It was taking up far too much room—and what unwelcome creatures did it harbor?

Jose Luis and Chayo slipped out to sleep in the van, Jose Luis and Carmen were invited to spend the night at the Comisario, and Dick and I walked back to Poncho and Luchita's, where mattresses had already been laid out—ours was in the kitchen. I slept like a rock, waking up just once to pull a red blanket over us because the mountain air had turned cool.

Before dawn Dick had the flashlight on, making coffee, but I just wanted to cover my eyes and make up for only three and a half hours of sleep the night before! I couldn't, though; I needed to wash up in the open-air facilities before the sun appeared if I wanted any privacy. How do they manage here without bathrooms? I wondered. "The swine are the sanitation workers," Alfonso quipped. "They're at hand even before a person has finished. They keep the village clean."

I was determined to wait till there was a bathroom. The pigs roamed everywhere, oinking and snorting over the sandy soil like vacuum cleaners. On one of the trips when Dick slept in the van, he was awakened by what he thought was an earthquake. A herd of hogs was rooting underneath and shaking the vehicle!

Alfonso had connected Luchita's new four-burner countertop stove the night before, and Dick said he'd make us a McDonald's breakfast. We did end up having scrambled eggs. And Luchita had me mix two cans of tuna fish with chopped tomato and onion. It was easy except for getting the tuna out without a can opener. Then I remembered from my youth, my mother teaching me how to do it with a paring knife. That saved the day.

The men gathered and formed a crew for moving the lumber. Luchita and I were busy scrubbing down the kitchen walls and floor and didn't pay attention until we heard shouting from the front room. Sra. Lucia had arrived, protesting the moving of her wood. Luchita went to investigate. Jose Luis and Chayo appeared in the kitchen, and we formed a prayer circle, asking the Lord to please intervene and bring peace. Luchita took Sra. Lucia aside and pointed out the benefits of the relocation. Some valuable lumber had begun to rot with the humidity that had seeped in. Besides that, tarantulas, scorpions, and spiders were having a heyday!

She went away happy and came back around at lunchtime and accepted our invitation to eat. Luchita made a pot of rice, and I fixed the sack of green beans I'd brought along. Poncho had asked us to bring vegetables because they are very scarce in the village.

Fifteen-year-old Saul who had come in the van with us had cleaned out the water cistern the day before, dipping out all the green water filled with leaves. Green tea, anyone? Today Alfonso scrubbed it with soap and water and then filled it with a hose from the neighbors. We had brown water now instead of green. I'd noticed coming up the mountain that the river was brown with the recent rains. During the first trip our church made to the Yoloxochitl there was drought, and the villagers had trekked to the top of the mountain to beg the Aztec god Tlaloc for rain. I inquired if the rains hadn't come anyhow because it was the rainy season, but they said no.

I wasn't aware till later that Alfonso had begun carrying water from his newly filled cistern all the way to the corner of the back yard, where there was a little structure with a toilet seat built in. He cleaned it up and got it ready for use. A bathroom! I had no idea one existed in the village. He showed it to us with pride. "Alfonso, your bathroom is fit for a king!" I told him. He grinned.

Luchita put a curtain over the entrance, carried buckets of water, and announced it was ready for anyone who wanted to bathe. The "shower" was the same as at Don Zenon's: a bucket of water with a bowl for a dipper to pour it over you.

In a way I felt I had already bathed that day. Perspiration poured from every pore as I worked, sweeping, mopping, putting up beds, and unpacking. I just relaxed and considered it a bath. When a fan got turned on inside the tiny house, my hair stuck out in every direction, blow-dried!

We ran out of bottled drinking water, so Dick went down to the village well with the comisario's daughter Kenya showing him the way and filled the five-gallon bottle with fresh water and lugged it back, panting. Ana Lidia (Poncho and Luchita's younger daughter) went too. They said the water was safe for drinking, but I waited. That night we bought bottles of cold water in a store on the way back from a meeting in the home of Aureliana.

I had gotten bathed and freshened up after all for the meeting and put on my embroidered Yoloxochitl dress Dick had bought me on his second trip here. The women of the village occupy themselves in embroidery work, and that is the main income in the village. Lots of people complimented me on the dress, and when we stopped in at Don Zenon's house afterward, his wife, Margarita, bent over and examined the stitching. "My daughter Guvelia made that dress," she exclaimed happily. "That's her embroidery style!" She was so pleased, knowing their daughter had made my dress, and it made me happy too!

Something began to happen that summer of 2002 when Alfonso Bautista and his family set up house in Yolo. They adapted to the way of life of the Mixteco Indians and lived among them. Four years later, in April of 2006, on another of several trips I made with leaders from our church, an elderly man from the village, Maximino, came into the Bautistas' house carrying a papaya he had grown and carefully tended. The next day he came back with another and said to Alfonso, "You are not like the ones who come and leave. You came and stayed. We like that about you."

A vibrant church has been born in Yolo. We worshiped with them that Sunday morning and shared in the communion service together in the Mixteco dialect of the Yoloxochitl. Alfonso and his wife and three children had uprooted themselves and replanted themselves out of love for the Savior and for one of the many remote, unreached ethnic groups of Mexico. My prayer for them is from Ephesians 3:17-19: that they all, *"being rooted and grounded in love, may be able to comprehend with all the saints what is the width and length and depth and height—to know the love of Christ which passes knowledge."* And one day before the throne of God, we will all worship together from every people and tribe and tongue and nation—even the Yoloxochitl.

* * *

Epilogue

Back To My Beginnings

My dream, if we ever returned to the United States, was to live in the country. I longed for open spaces. I wanted to build a little house in Sugar Grove, where I was born, or live somewhere outside of town. I had been a city girl for fifty years, and now my rural roots were beckoning me. Nothing materialized, however.

Now again I was feeling starved and also squashed by city life, and I longed for nature and sunsets and solitude and space. I pored over that verse, *"He brought them out into a large place."* That's my verse! In that large place, I find what my soul and spirit are yearning for.

We had been looking at houses, and each was more unsatisfying that the one before it.

"Lord, You said that if we left house and land for You and Your kingdom's sake, You'd give us a hundred times more in this present life, with persecutions, and in the world to come everlasting life. Please *give,* Lord, out of Your riches in glory."

Then I remembered the time we had searched everywhere, unsuccessfully, and He had spoken to me, *"I am your house."*

"Jesus! You are my large place. I find all I need and infinitely more in You. I throw off the bonds of cramped and close and cluttered, and I breathe deeply of the free celestial air with all the beauty that surrounds You."

"You can live in the den," my mother said.

When Mother's boarders moved out of the little rooms Daddy had built onto the house, it was a convenient place for us to live, since we were helping prepare her meals and care for her. "I'm glad you decided to stay there," Jonita, the pastor's wife, said to me. "It's a gift to her." Jonita was right. And it was in my heart also, because I had not had significant time with her since I'd left home at age seventeen to study in Chicago.

Christmas of 2006 happened, and New Year's happened, with my not being overly impressed by either one. What's gone wrong with Christmas in the USA? Are people afraid to celebrate it? Is it unpopular or outlawed? Radio and TV didn't celebrate. It even got downplayed at our Baptist Church in Ione. Joyce had a CD of carols in the car, bless her heart. For some reason one stanza of "It Came Upon a Midnight Clear" struck me each time it came back around.

And ye beneath life's crushing load,
Whose forms are bending low,
Who toil along the climbing way
With painful steps and slow
Look now! For glad and golden hours
Come swiftly on the wing:
O rest beside the weary road
And hear the angels sing.

What touched me deeply was, *"O rest beside the weary road and hear the angels sing."* Tears come to my eyes now as I remember it—weariness, the need to rest, to hear the music. I'll rest beside you, weary road, and keep you company.

I was into erratic sleep patterns—waking up a 1:00 a.m. and not falling back asleep or waking up for three hours and finally falling back to sleep. This hasn't totally stopped. In today's wee hours I lay wide-eyed from 1:30 to 4:30 before returning to dream. Was I depressed? Were my days so filled with the demands of others that I had to grab alone time after midnight? Maybe some of both. I've got to have periods of solitude to think, assimilate, ponder, and reflect, and I'm wondering if when all my daytime minutes are snatched away like highway robbery with unending people and activity, accompanied by noise and clatter, my mind charges the bill during the dark hours of the night.

I can see now that much of what I experienced was the shock of reentry into my own culture after being away most of my lifetime. Things had changed, and I had a lot of catching up to do. I was different too and needed to unlearn many of the ways things are done in Mexico. In some areas I didn't fit in and felt like an outsider. I wasn't "in the know" in a number of aspects and had to humble myself and become a learner.

Dick and I lived in the den four years and helped look after Mama. How quickly the time went by. We got involved in the local church in teaching and outreaches, made trips back to Mexico and other places, and had special times with our three sons and their families.

I had been walking around the track in the park behind Christian Chapel in Tulsa. I was there with Linda that weekend of March 2010 for the Extraordinary Women conference at ORU. It was Sunday noon, and I pulled out my cell phone to call Mama. Joyce was sitting with her while our nephew Mike, her main caregiver, had gone for a short walk at Joyce's suggestion.

I sat down at a picnic table beside the walking path and chatted with Mama. She had enjoyed her lunch, and Joyce was sitting in the other living room recliner beside hers. When we finished I said goodbye with, "I love you, Mama."

Her sweet voice replied, "I love you, too, Helen."

Those were her exact words, the last I ever heard her say, because about two hours later Joyce called to say our mother had slipped quietly into the presence of Jesus with a slight guttural noise. When Joyce heard the sound and turned to look, she was already gone. Gently, quietly, Jesus must have called her name, and she responded—just like that. *She had walked with Him all her life.*

I'm in my seventies now.

My sister Joyce, my Aunt Lois, and I drive up to the little church in Sugar Grove where my parents first gave their hearts to Jesus when I was six months old. It sits alone on a dirt road—a little church in the wildwood. The doors are locked, so I walk all the way around it.

It went through a fire since I was here with my parents for their fortieth anniversary. The superstructure has been rebuilt. That happens sometimes in our lives, too: fires of testing. The foundation remains secure though.

I cross the unpaved road, jump the ditch, and walk up the slope to where my grandparents lived. The house is gone, and they have all gone on ahead, too, my parents and grandparents, their journey ended.

I pluck up a tiny pine tree and bring it back to the car.

My journey continues.

I'm eager for what's yet to come.

* * *

IF I COULD JUST IMAGINE...

Suddenly I'm there—my hope and dream and longing of a lifetime—standing before Jesus, King of Kings, Lord of Lords, my Redeemer God.

"Well done," He says. The words wash over my spirit like a healing balm, and the warmth flowing from His eyes melts my heart like sunshine on butter. His very presence envelopes me in a loving embrace.

"Jesus, my Lord and my God," I breathe. "All of my life, I've been looking for You."

"I know," He says. "I created you with a longing for Me. Before you were conceived in the womb, you were already conceived in my mind and heart. Before I made you, I called you to be my witness to the nations. Come on in. I've got a lot of surprises for you."

I knew my journey's end was only the beginning.

* * *